VINTAGE HOME

Sarah Moore

VINTAGE HOME

*Stylish ideas and over 50
handmade projects from
furniture to decorating*

Sarah Moore

PHOTOGRAPHY BY DEBI TRELOAR

To my lovely family

First published in Great Britain in 2013 by Kyle Books
an imprint of Kyle Cathie Limited
67–69 Whitfield Street
London W1T 4HF
general.enquiries@kylebooks.com
www.kylebooks.com

ISBN: 978 0 85783 142 2

A CIP catalogue record for this title is available from the British Library

Editor: Vicky Orchard
Design: Victoria Sawdon
Photography: Debi Treloar
Copy editor: Salima Hirani
Production: Lisa Pinnell

Colour reproduction by ALTA London
Printed and bound in the UK by Butler Tanner & Dennis

Contents

Just my cup of tea

Squeezed into the pages of this book is an eclectic mix of vintage styling, projects to make, decorating ideas, practical instructions and, I hope, a little inspiration to help you make the most of the abundant vintage items that are available from vintage dealers, online auctions, charity shops, car boot sales, reclamation yards, flea markets, antique dealers, house clearances and vintage fairs.

MAKING GOOD USE OF THE THINGS THAT YOU FIND

Seeking out old stuff for your home can be time consuming, but there are a number of advantages to using vintage materials when decorating and making objects for your home. Sometimes, just for the price of a latte, you might find a pair of perfect curtains, a length of fabric with a pretty print or a small box of beautiful buttons. As you build your collection of thrifty and gorgeous vintage finds, you can customise them and decorate your entire home at a fraction of the cost of buying things new. The recycling – or upcycling – element involved in this process has a feel-good factor, too. Giving a new lease of life to homewares that might otherwise have been heading for the bonfire or landfill is good for the planet as well as the pocket. Everyone can find their own take on vintage style and pluck pieces from any era they fancy. If you love a rummage, cannot pass a market without popping in, or if you do not mind rifling through the rails in charity shops or even perusing the odd skip (ask before you take!) you can get a huge amount of pleasure from finding just the right materials to add colour, character and individuality to your home.

A LITTLE OF WHAT YOU FANCY

You can slot just a little bit of vintage into your house – a fine bone china tea set or string of wallpaper chains, for instance – or you can fall in, head first, and fill your entire home, from cellar to ceiling, walls to wardrobe, with your vintage finds. If you are not quite sure which direction to head in, have a look at the one thing four ways projects to get an idea of the different options or go to a couple of antique fairs or vintage markets and have a really good look and think before you buy. I hope you like this book and that vintage style is just your cup of tea, too!

Buying and using old stuff

If you select vintage fabrics and linens, wallpapers and furniture wisely, and know how to make the best of each item you have acquired, you can use your precious finds to give your home a gorgeous vintage vibe without breaking the bank.

FABRIC

Bolts and yardage of unused vintage fabrics do still appear on the market. Some are dead stock that was never sold, other bits were purchased but never made up into the projects intended. If you can lay your hands on enough yards to cover your sofa, make a room's worth of curtains or a whole set of bedding, that is a very lucky find indeed, so reclaiming fabric is a good alternative.

The advantage of making up projects in previously used fabrics is that your makes look instantly at home in vintage-style houses. If they are no longer usable in their current state, curtains and bedding provide large pieces of fabric that can be carefully trimmed and unpicked to produce workable pieces of fabric.

If you are buying secondhand, give everything a good wash in a colour-kind washing powder and iron it before you begin. Hold woollen fabrics up to the light to check for areas of wear that might cause problems after making. Think carefully before cutting up precious fabrics, keeping in mind the old expression, 'measure twice, cut once' to minimise wastage.

And there is no reason why you should not mix and match new fabrics with old. New fabrics with a traditional twist work best for this approach. Striped ticking or plain dyed linen and calico sit really well alongside old fabrics, making them ideal to use for linings, allowing you to make your vintage fabrics go twice as far. Ironing and pinning projects well helps to keep everything aligned, so put up your ironing board every time you get out your sewing machine and you will be amazed by how much straighter and neater your projects turn out.

HOUSEHOLD LINENS AND BEDDING

Bottom drawers and airing cupboards, trunks and attics, armoires and chests of drawers were stuffed full of beautiful linens only one hundred years ago in houses up and down the country. Monograms and laundry marks are still found on many old pieces of table and bed linen as a reminder of how carefully they were created, looked after and kept. Today, these vintage pieces provide a useful source of large-scale linens, cottons and fabrics to use in projects and around the house.

If you come across a lovely linen sheet or a tablecloth in good condition, do not cut it up or use it in anything other than its whole state. But find a flawed example that is marked, ripped or holey and I would suggest in a second that you cut it up. And dye it and use the trim, embroidery or monogram.

Buying secondhand sheets and household linens might not be your cup of tea, but a clean, ironed old sheet or cloth is a joy to use, so if you find some beautiful bits and pieces whilst out shopping, wash them well or have them cleaned professionally, air them on the line, then wash and press them again and you can normally rid them of any old or musty smells and make them feel like they are your own. Use linen water (see page 46) to make them smell lovely, too.

Investigate the fabrics you find to ensure they are made with natural fibres. Linen is cold to the touch and crumples easily, while cotton is a little softer. Avoid buying anything that does not crease when you scrunch it as it may be a synthetic fabric, which will not dye or sew up in quite the same way as a vintage fabric, producing results with a different feel to those you are after.

FURNITURE

Sturdy, old-fashioned pieces of furniture are great workhorses for family living, and if you are looking for a good buy, it is worth noting that there is a little window between a piece of furniture being secondhand and it becoming a vintage piece. So if you spot, for instance, a well-made chest of drawers or a wardrobe that has never been a flat-pack, and the piece has not as yet slipped into iconic or antique status, you can nab yourself a bargain in the right buying environment.

House clearances and junk shops can produce such finds, and if they are not pretty enough in their original state, there are heaps of options for transforming outdated furniture into lovely pieces for your home. At the other end of the spectrum you can pick up the proper stuff at auction houses. Fine antiques, fashionable shapes and perfect examples are best left unpainted, wallpapered or distressed.

Whatever your price range, you must ensure the furniture is safe and sound. Look out for woodworm holes, particularly those with fine dust coming from them, as this is a sign of active worms. This condition can be treated, but make sure you do so before bringing any offending articles into your home to infect wooden floors or other furniture. Check that the joints of chairs are solid, that hinges and locks are in good working order and that there are no loose splinters or sticking-out nails. Take a tape measure out with you so you know that your purchase will fit into its new home or your car – cheap wardrobes can be expensive by the time you have paid for delivery. We have a fantastic antique cherry wood cupboard in our garage that is too big for our house and it had to be delivered by truck, so I speak from experience. Lovely cupboard, though.

All in all, you just need to bear in mind that buying secondhand has a slightly different set of rules. It is generally cheaper, but the responsibility lies with you to make very sure you are happy before you purchase as markets and boot sales rarely offer returns. Have faith, though – you could always hold a garage sale and perhaps recoup your costs... cherry wood cupboard, anyone?

sourcing vintage

Ardent fans of vintage items can scan a stall in seconds and know if they have discovered a rich vein of ephemera, fabric or homeware that tickles their fancy or that they should walk quickly on to the next place. Finding your own particular style with vintage may be the work of a moment or an ever-changing conundrum, but the really great thing about buying old stuff is the variety available to suit every budget, style and look you can think of. Choosing where and how to shop is fun, too.

Getting down and dirty and peering through boxes of house-clearance fodder is at the grittier end of the spectrum and car-boot sales and markets up and down the country are great places to pick up some real bargains that have usually had only one careful owner. You have to be up early and ready to do battle if you want to get there before dealers, shop owners and other vintage enthusiasts. It is not unusual to see people sprinting across markets as they open, running towards a piece of turquoise glass, or a spotty dress or picture they cannot live without. It can be quite an eye opener to be caught up in one of these stampedes and the pickings can be rich indeed. Best buys from general boot sales include kitchenalia, bedding, curtains, small pieces of furniture, household china and gardenware. Price tags are unusual and even though I always test the water cautiously, haggling is usually acceptable and even expected. Cash only is the rule.

Charity, thrift and junk shops usually have a more sanitised offering, so you are less likely to have to trawl through an entire house contents to find your materials in these often-rich sources of vintage items. Most charity shops have more on offer than first meets the eye, so do not be afraid to ask if there is a particular something that you are looking for. Many have boxes of buttons, broken jewellery, fabric scraps or old linens that are not on show.

And it is always worth asking if the shop will save pieces just for you that might not appeal to all or cannot be sold generally, but can offer a rich source of materials for the homemaker, such as holey cashmere jumpers (for making into blankets), broken china (to use for mosaics), damaged vintage clothes or curtains and bedding that is no longer usable (from which to reclaim fabric).

ANTIQUE AND VINTAGE MARKETS

Dealers and collectors, amateur and professional, buy and sell at organised venues and specialist fairs and if you conduct a little research into fairs in your local area, you are likely to find one that suits your style. Look for fabric rummages, book fairs, vintage and seasonal markets and big fairs at major exhibition centres and showgrounds as these would be well worth visiting. You could find specialist textiles, old linens, antique furniture, china, glassware and handmade vintage-style pieces amongst the long list of vintage items available at such locations and events.

Larger fairs may hold a trade day on the opening day and open the event to the general public afterwards. Amazing bargains can be had on the first days as occasional undetected treasures come to market, and on last days when the thought of selling is more appealing to the trader than the thought of packing everything up.

In general, prices will be cheaper here than on the high street. Ask for the best price and, if you are interested in more than one item on any stall, ask for a discount. Again, only cash is usually taken at such events, but sometimes credit cards are accepted.

AUCTION HOUSES

Auction houses are often perceived as intimidating, cliquey places with an etiquette and set of rules all of their own, but they are well worth visiting. They are particularly good places to go to pick up large pieces of furniture, paintings or treasures, or if you have a house to fill. Auction houses normally publish a calendar with details of types of sales across the year. For larger sales, there will be several viewing days before the buying days, when you can go and see all that is on offer, or view online, before the lots finally come under the hammer. Country auctions might be as casual as a few lines of boxes in a field.

If you want to go to a proper sale and bid on an item or two, you will need to register for a bidding number that confirms your details and enters you into a binding contract to pay for the lot you have won. There are estimates and guide prices at some auction houses to give you a rough idea of what things might cost. Reserves are the lowest price that the item will sell for, so if bids do not raise to that price the piece will remain unsold. If you cannot make it to the auction itself, or you think you might get carried away by the bidding process, you can leave a commission bid stating the most you would like to pay for an item. The auctioneer will bid on your behalf up to the maximum figure you have stated. If the item comes in below your bid then you pay one bid above your closest competition. This addition is the amount that each bid is increased by during the auction. Pay careful attention to the fees payable at each auction house as the winning bids are subject to an extra percentage charge known as a buyer's premium, generally between 10 and 20 per cent. Sellers also pay a similar commission to the auction house and these prices may also be subject to further taxes. Charges vary from one auction house to the next.

Once you understand how they work, and any intimidation you might have felt has passed, you can have a fun day out at an auction house as you witness lots rocket way over their estimates or find yourself taking away a bookshelf or a chair that you had suddenly decided you needed as it cost less than the bacon roll you had just eaten for lunch.

ONLINE AUCTIONS

If you know exactly what you are looking for, online auctions can be great places to find it. Listings for vintage items are huge in number. Stealthily bidding for your favourite stuff can be done from the comfort of your armchair and delivered to your door at only the click of a button. Keep an eye out for your best bits and relist anything you buy in error!

RECLAMATION YARDS

For pretty tiles or fireplaces, big old bathtubs and old-fashioned radiators, a trip to a reclamation yard might be the order of the day. They range from super smart cavernous barns and buildings filled with copper baths and Georgian panelling to hardly-able-to-get-through-the-gate hoarders' paradises. Good for larger pieces and architectural gardenware, there is often a beauty in the utility of what is sold at reclamation yards. If you are undertaking building work and want to add or reinstate period features in your home, a reclamation yard is definitely the kind of place you need to visit. Smart business like places should have prices on most pieces, but those with green grass and weeds growing through them may be priced in a way that makes you think the owners are reluctant to sell. School, church and factory fittings turn up in reclamation yards alongside domestic pieces.

VINTAGE SHOPS AND ONLINE EMPORIUMS

Vintage has a growing following. I tacked my flag to a vintage pole a very long time ago and it has been great to see the momentum gathering as more and more markets, fairs, shops and online stores have opened up to satisfy the baying vintage-loving crowds. Cherry-picked and polished, most of the items in such outlets have to be in cracking condition to make it onto the market. Expect to pay more than you would at a market or car-boot sale and relish the fact that someone else has been up at dawn, driven for miles, sprinted across the market, taken it home, cleaned, polished and mended it and popped it in their civilised shop. As with all vintage items, if you see something amazing and it is close enough to your budget, buy it now as the chances are it will be gone tomorrow.

WHAT TO LOOK OUT FOR

Cost aside, whatever you buy, whether remotely or face-to-face, you need to make sure that it is sound, safe and suitable for your needs. Rolls of old wallpaper need to be pliable enough to still unroll and be stuck to the walls. Fabrics need to be strong and unfaded in the main so that they can withstand the process of cutting, sewing and usage afterwards. Furniture can have woodworm, rot or be painted in thick lead paint. So seek professional advice if you buy something that is not quite as perfect as you once thought. Woodworm can be treated, and weak joints can be glued and pinned back in place, but anything covered with thick lead paint should be either sent away to be stripped professionally or totally covered without sanding or chipping in case particles are ingested.

Think carefully before handing out old toys to young children as health and safety regulations were not as sensitive in bygone years. And remember not to get carried away with a bargain. An ugly shape and clunky styling will still look the same even after you have painted, waxed, stripped or polished it.

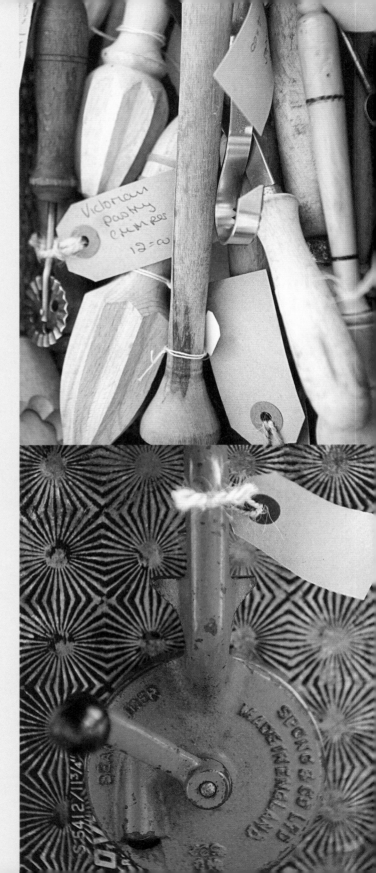

Vintage equipment

This is not a definitive list of everything that you will need, but a small selection of the tools that we used in the projects. Most of the DIY in our house starts by looking in the utensil pot in the kitchen in the vain hope that there will be some screwdrivers or a small hammer amongst the spoons. Gathering together a few proper pieces of kit and keeping them together saves time.

GENERAL PROJECTS

hand drill

screwdrivers

hand saw

hammer

nails

craft knife

tape measure

sewing machine

needles and threads

paper for templates

scissors

pencil for marking

stamps and inks

WALLPAPERING

table

brushes for pasting and smoothing

pot for paste

metal ruler

large scissors

large sponge for smoothing

little roller for pasting down edges

CHALK PAINTING

chalk paint

brushes

dust sheets

sandpaper

wire wool

dark and light wax

soft cloths

scrapers

VINTAGE WALLPAPER

I have a passion for old wallpapers, from the tiniest scraps to the Holy Grail of vintage wallpaper finds – rolls and rolls of one pattern of proper vintage paper. Old wallpaper used to be rolled with the pattern on the inside and required trimming before use, so you always know you are on to a winner if you spot these telltale vintage wallpaper credentials.

For small projects and patchworking, condition is not hugely important. But if you plan to paper a wall or an entire room, ensure the paper is not too brittle or fragile to withstand the pasting and cutting required.

The surface you will be papering must be a clean and dust-free surface that has either been covered with lining paper or is smooth enough to produce a good finish once papered. Brush down the walls before you begin. Invest in a pair of long scissors, good-quality wallpaper brushes and a wallpaper table. Several attempts to paper from the floor have resulted in a bad back, bruised knees and a sudden desire to cut the whole-room project to a feature-wall size. Buy the table – it is worth every penny.

BELOW ARE SOME BASIC RULES TO BEAR IN MIND WHEN APPROACHING A WALLPAPERING PROJECT:

- allow for the repeat in the pattern when buying paper as this may mean you use up more than you think. Cut the amount you need to cover a wall, allowing for the repeats, before you start pasting

- always paste the paper and not the wall

- smooth the paper evenly and gently in place, lining up the pattern as you hang

- you can purchase little rollers for pressing down the edges of the paper once it has been pasted in place, and special strong glue for sticking down any loose pieces. These are both valuable pieces of kit.

Occasionally, you can still find vintage wallpaper trimmers for trimming old papers with trimming lines, or you can paper the wall with the borders still in place if you prefer not to try to trim them with a craft knife or scissors. Some old papers have an almost chalky texture and some of the printed colours may run or smudge, so test an area to see how it handles. Some of the most expensive vintage papers still cost less than their modern equivalents, so if you are lucky enough to find a big batch of lovely paper it might be worth getting a professional to hang it so you know the end result will be perfect.

Remember – it is easier to apply wallpaper in smaller pieces, so try a patchworking project (see page 101) if precision hanging sounds out of your league.

Furniture painting

If you have not tried a restoration or refurbishment project before, look out for smaller pieces on which to cut your teeth. Pot cupboards or little bathroom cabinets, side tables and blanket boxes are of just the right scale for getting started and gaining some instant gratification. If you are planning to enhance anything passed down in your family, make sure you are about to paper the inside of a cheap and cheerful piece of furniture rather than a rare Georgian one and seek professional advice before attacking your granny's armoire if in any doubt.

There are all sorts of paints available but for a vintage finish chalk paint is very forgiving, easy to use, non-toxic and you can mix colours together to produce your own perfect shade. It can be painted over any finish without sanding or preparation and, for a vintage look, this is great news.

Use masking tape to cover up any areas of the piece that you don't want to paint and remove any knobs or handles to make the process easier.

Brush the surface of the piece all over first to remove any loose flakes of paint or dust. Mix the paint really well so that it has a smooth creamy consistency and then, using a nice fat brush, start to apply the paint - apply an even layer over the whole area you want to cover and allow it to dry. This will take at least a couple of hours.

Waxing: for a simple finish, just use a soft cloth or a clean paintbrush to apply a layer of clear wax over the whole piece.

Distressing: favourite word of shabby chic advocaters everywhere, this is the process of making new stuff look old. Use scrapers and sandpaper for roughing up the painted surface. Apply other layers of slightly different coloured paint to make it look like the piece has been painted several times. allowing it to dry in between, and scraping and scuffing through various different layers of paint as you go.

When you have achieved the look you are after you can finish off the whole piece with a coat of soft, clear wax, applied with a cloth or clean paintbrush or apply dark treacle-coloured wax to edges and areas to darken the surface for an instant lived-in vintage look.

PRETTY
AND
PRACTICAL

Kitchen organisation

In my dream larder there are mesmerising rows of provisions in neatly arranged lines. The pristine shelves, finished with pretty edging, are packed full of jars of gleaming apple jellies topped with frilly chintz, a whole honeycomb floating in a jar of amber honey and bags of Arborio rice, pudding rice and Basmati rice. The coffee comes in canisters and the tea, in pretty tins. Reusable jars have labels made of blackboard paint on which to write their changing contents. When you walk into the kitchen you smell gathered herbs drying in hanging baskets. On a cabinet you see a slab of marble on which a big chunk of Cheddar cheese is kept cold, a fat Stilton sitting stoutly under a huge majolica cheese jar and little netted frames covering perfect pies. An impressive ham hangs from a beam in a cool corner, and a meat safe reveals a splendid rib of beef through its tight netting. In this shrine to culinary order, no one has dared to put away a sticky jar of honey, or stashed a vinegar with the oils...

The reality is somewhat more sparse and less glorious. No walk-in pantry or chilled game larder for me - instead, I make do with an old painted storecupboard. I am still saving up for a ham and there is a sticky honey jar right next to the mustard. And a massive jar of Marmite eerily hurtles from the top shelf on a regular basis.

But order can be brought to such frugal places. For instance, the blackboard-paint-labels-on-jars business is very easily done. The odd drawstring bag is achievable too. Make getting the porridge a pleasure and put some order into your supplies.

JAR LABELS

Use a dark chalk paint and paint it onto a square area on the side of the jar - use masking tape to mask the rest of the jar and help you give the painted square crisp edges. Allow the paint to dry before peeling off the tape. Use blackboard chalks to write and rewrite the labels.

DRAWSTRING BAGS

These are very easy to make (see page 114). For your pantry or cupboard, make a selection of bags in a variety of ticking stripes. Add a tiny pocket for the label and use-by date of any contents.

FURTHER IDEAS

Use decanters sourced from charity shops or old beer and lemonade bottles with a swing top for oils and vinegars and search out fab old Kilner jars.

Adding those pretty circular frills to jar tops makes rows of jars a joy to look at.

Tip out plastic-lidded spices into little tins with clear lids and top with a label.

Make yourself a little blackboard frame for the back of the cupboard door or chalk paint a door panel on the inside of the cupboard – and write something useful on it. Mine says, 'Mind your head, here comes the Marmite!'

Colander vegetable hangers

Vegetables, dried herbs, eggs and fruit all love to be kept somewhere airy and out of the way of small hands or pets. A stack of vintage enamel colanders looks lovely hanging from beams or ceilings, and provides a useful extra space if storage is not abundant in your kitchen. Your collection can be all the same size or a graduating set, and you can add as many colander layers as you like. You can use strong twine or fine rope to suspend them and you will need a secure hook attached to your ceiling or an exposed beam for hanging. Seek advice if you are not sure how to locate a suitably robust point on your ceiling from which to suspend your hook.

1. Arange the colanders with the smallest at the top and then start to thread. Cut three lengths of twine the same length and then thread the twine through a hole in the bottom colander, outside to in, and tie a large knot to stop the twine from slipping through the hole. Repeat with the other pieces of twine.

2. Measure an even distance up the rope then make another knot at the same height on each rope. Add the second colander, feeding the twine into the holes from the outside in. Make sure that it is hanging straight by holding it up and adjusting the position if necessary. Add any more colanders in the same way and finish by tying the three pieces of twine together in a secure knot.

3. Screw the hook into the appropriate area on the ceiling and hang the colander stack from it. Do not overfill the colanders or place anything too heavy in them.

YOU WILL NEED:

....

WOODEN MOUNT * TAPE MEASURE * PENCIL * THICK WIRE
(FINE COAT HANGERS ARE A GREAT SOURCE) * HAND-HELD
DRILL AND DRILL BIT THE SAME THICKNESS AS YOUR WIRE
* PAINT AND PAINTBRUSH (OPTIONAL) * PICTURE HOOK
AND FASTENING * PLIERS WITH WIRE CUTTERS * STRING
* WOOLLEN OR THICK UPHOLSTERY FABRIC * FABRIC
SCISSORS * GLUE GUN * NEEDLE AND THREAD

Antler hatstands

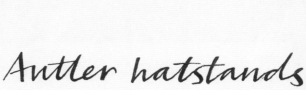

Not the most obvious vintage home project, but I have always wanted a massive pair of antlers on which to hang our hats, or one pair for each family member, hung at just the right height for them. These faux antlers, made of wire bound in fabric, take a little bit of making, but are well worth the effort. You need an impressive-looking mount for your antlers – taxidermy suppliers sell appropriate shields and boards that are very reasonably priced, or you can sand and paint an offcut of wood, a slice of tree trunk, a piece of driftwood or even an old chopping board to make your mount.

1. Mark a cross on the mount where each antler will be. Choose the number of wires you will be using, allowing one wire for every point that you want on your antlers. A maximum of five is probably best. For a single point antler use double wire to add strength. Check that you have the right size drill bit so the wire just fits in the hole and then drill the right number of holes around the crosses, only a couple of millimetres apart, all the way through to the back, making sure that you have a suitable surface behind that you can drill into. Finish your mount with paint if required and add a strong picture hook to the back for hanging.

2. If you are using coat hangers clip off the twisted ends and straighten them out. Chop the wire into different lengths and line them all up at one end. Use some string to bind all the wires for one antler together at this end, leaving about 2cm bare so they can be pushed into the holes in the mount.

3. Bend the wires into antler shapes, tying the wires together by wrapping more string around the bundle just before each point forks off. Make the antlers as a mirror of each other so they make a matching pair.

4. Start to bind the frames with long strips of fabrics, all cut into 1–2cm wide strips. Use a glue gun or sew the end of the strip to the wires, then wind it around and around the antler, moving up towards the points. Sew or glue each strip in place and keep winding until all the wire is covered. Leave the mount end of the wires free from fabric so they can slot into the holes in the mount.

5. When you have a balanced pair of antlers, feed the wires into the holes in the mount with plenty of hot glue and cover with a little more fabric to hide the glue. Hang on the wall as decoration, or use as a hat stand.

YOU WILL NEED:

TAPE MEASURE * FABRIC * TAILOR'S CHALK OR FABRIC MARKER * FABRIC SCISSORS * IRON * PINS * SEWING MACHINE * SEWING THREAD * RIBBONS * SAFETY PIN

Shoebags

To paraphrase William Morris, don't have anything in your house that you know not to be beautiful or useful. There is no better way to while away a quiet evening than to make useful objects for your home, such as covers for your hangers and bags to protect your best shoes. These handy items must have been made in their multitudes in times past as I still find lovely hanger covers or the occasional embroidered shoe bag on my vintage-buying forays, and they can be put to good use in a modern home. My dream wardrobe would be full of shoes carefully padded out with beautifully made little wooden shoe trees, swirly dresses swishing on covered hangers and shiny patent toes poking from the tops of these pretty little bags.

1. Measure out some rectangles of fabric that are each around 30cm x 40cm or large enough to easily cover your party shoes when folded in half along the longer edges. Chalk and then cut them out.

2. Fold over a hem of about 2cm along one of the long edges of each fabric rectangle, then iron and pin it in place. Sew along the hem, removing the pins as you go. Fold each rectangle in half along the longer edges with the right sides facing and the hemmed edge at one end - this will be the top end of the bag. Pin the edges. Sew the bottom edge and nearly all of the side edge together, using a 1cm seam allowance, leaving just the hemmed area unsewn.

3. Turn the bags so that their right sides are facing out, push out all the corners, then iron them carefully. Thread a ribbon onto a safety pin and push it into one of the openings of the hem at the top of a bag, along the channel and pull it out of the opening at the other end of the hem. Ensure that there is an equal amount of ribbon emerging from each side of the channel. Tie the ends of the drawstring in a simple knot. Repeat with each rectangle. Fill each bag with a pair of your best shoes.

YOU WILL NEED:

OLD EMBROIDERED TABLECLOTHS OR PRETTY
FABRIC * HANGERS * TAILOR'S CHALK * FABRIC
SCISSORS * PINS * IRON * SEWING MACHINE
* SEWING THREAD

Hanger covers

*As if knitting or crocheting hanger covers was not
enough, these little slip covers are perfect for keeping
best dresses and twinsets in peak condition.*

1. Lay out the fabric with the right side facing down. You will
use your hangers as templates for the top curved seams of the
covers. If your hangers are all the same shape, you can use just
one hanger as a template. Lay it on the fabric and chalk its
outline, extending the sides down from the base of the hanger
by about 10cm to make a little cape shape. Cut around the
shape you have drawn about 2cm from the chalk line, then use
this piece of fabric as a template to make an identical piece for
the back of the hanger cover.

2. Turn over a 1cm hem on the bottom edge of each piece of fabric
and pin it in place. Iron the hem, then sew along it, removing
the pins as you go. Align two hemmed pieces with their right
sides facing, and pin them together. Sew up along a side edge
and along the curve to the top of the cover until you reach the
point at which the hook will pass through the cover, working
with a 1cm seam allowance and removing the pins as you sew.
Leave a 1cm gap for passing the hook of the hanger through the
cover. Continue from the other side of the gap down along the
other side edge of the cover. The bottom hemmed edge remains
unsewn. Trim away a little of the excess fabric at the point at
which the hook will pass through the cover, and turn the cover
so that the right sides are facing out. Iron the cover, then pop
it over a hanger. Repeat the process until all your hangers are
covered then use these for your best dresses.

PRETTY AND PRACTICAL

Little dress peg bags

Simple and sweet, small-dress peg bags make charming reminders of younger days if all the little ones in your life have grown out of their first outfits and have moved on to bigger things.

1. Turn the dress inside out and line up the bottom hem. Pin it closed, checking that the seams are even at the sides. Using running stitch, sew across the hems on your sewing machine, removing the pins as you go.

2. Sew the cuffs in the same way so that the ends of the sleeves are stitched together too. Turn the dress out through the neck so that the right sides are facing out.

3. Pop the hanger into the neck opening and hand-sew around the hanger and into the back of the dress at a couple of points to hold the hanger securely in place. Use the neck opening to fill the newly created pocket inside the dress with pegs and hang it on the washing line when you hang out the washing, sliding it along the line with you as you go.

Apple crate storage

These fabulous wooden crates are ideal for flexible storage. Robust enough to stack, they have a utilitarian style that is simple and relaxed - so filling them with your pile of shoes by the back door is just fine. Apple crates are still available in the kind of quantities that makes you marvel at how many orchards and fruit farms there must once have been.

Such is my enthusiasm for an apple crate or two, I shipped a quantity over from France. There seemed to be an eclipse as the articulated lorry reversed close to our cottage, and lots of beeping as the forklift truck lowered down the pallets of carefully wrapped orchard plunder. They have all been really useful, but only recently the memory of the beeping and partial eclipse stopped me committing to buy 500 very reasonably priced vintage potato crates. You can have too much of a good thing, you know!

Buy with care if you are purchasing a single crate. Check it for woodworm and loose or broken panels or splits and splinters. If you are shipping in a van-load of crates you have not had a chance to inspect, you might need to take a little bit of rough with the smooth and treat or mend any crate that is not in great condition.

These useful crates can be put to good use in the home. Have a look at page 157 to see how to transform an apple crate into a bedside table, or if you like the shoe-box idea, buy a set of four casters with screw-in fixings to attach wheels to your box.

Apple crates do make perfect shelving. If you would prefer a cleaner interior, use masking tape to mask the entire exterior of the box so that no paint can escape between the slats onto the exterior, then paint the inside of the crate with chalk paint. Remove the tape when the paint is thoroughly dry. Paint the interiors in a range of colours and use colour coding to encourage the less tidy people in your life to put things back in their proper places - dressing up clothes into the blue box, power tools into the pink one, and so on.

Another idea is to take your apple crates into the garden to use as little tables for summer sitting, or you could actually use them for storing apples, carefully wrapping the fruit in newspaper before loading them into the crates and storing in a cool, dry place.

YOU WILL NEED:

OLD CUPBOARD * SANDPAPER * MASKING TAPE * CHALK
PAINT * PAINTBRUSHES * CLEAR WAX AND DARK WAX * TAPE
MEASURE * WALLPAPER OR BROWN PAPER * PENCIL * RULER
* PAPER SCISSORS * LARGE COIN OR LITTLE EGG CUP FOR
SCALLOP TEMPLATE * PVA GLUE

Paper - lined cupboard

At home we keep our cups in a cupboard that sits on the work surface, a little pine cupboard that someone had varnished a tricky orange that we lived with for half a decade. This cupboard was practical in size and shape but the colour was far from easy on the eye and it was right in the heart of the kitchen, where we spend the most time. The answer to this problem was simple - I painted the cupboard and lined the interior, covering over the orange entirely. Pieces of furniture like this are a joy to update and every morning I look at the paper lining with its pretty scalloped edges and love the piece afresh.

1. Before you start painting, check over your furniture carefully and sand away splinters or loose flakes of paint. Avoid sanding or chipping off old lead paint, which looks thick and glossy, as this is toxic. It should be removed professionally or painted over completely. Mask any handles, keyholes or hinges that you would like to keep in their original state.

2. Give the outside of the cupboard a good coat of chalk paint all over. Allow it to dry thoroughly before opening the cupboard to paint any parts of the interior that you would like painted rather than papered. If you are painting the inside in a different colour, use easy-peel masking tape to mask the edges of the freshly painted exterior surfaces for a crisp finish. Paint the interior areas and allow to dry thoroughly.

3. Remove the masking tape when the paint is completely dry and add a layer of clear wax to the painted areas with a clean, dry brush to seal the surface of the slightly porous paint.

4. Measure the areas of the interior that you would like to paper (such as shelves or the back or sides of the cupboard), then transfer these dimensions to the back of your wallpaper using a pencil and ruler. Now cut out the shapes. For a shelf consider adding a prettily scalloped front edge to the paper. Draw around an egg cup or a large coin to mark out a series of half circles on the back of the paper as a cutting guide, then cut the scalloped edge.

5. Use PVA glue and a brush to cover the areas of the cupboard interior you wish to paper in a thin layer of glue. Press the paper in place and smooth out any bubbles.

6. If you like a smart and crisp finish, your cupboard should be finished at this point. For a distressed and slightly older feeling, sand and chip back the paint from any edges and raised features on the cupboard. A little dark wax worked into the cracks and lines on the paint helps to achieve a lived-in look too.

YOU WILL NEED:

IRONING BOARD * HEAVY-WEIGHT UPHOLSTERY FABRIC
* TAILOR'S CHALK * FABRIC SCISSORS * PINS * IRON
* SEWING MACHINE * SEWING THREAD * LARGE SAFETY
PIN * A LENGTH OF STRONG STRING OR TAPE THAT IS
OVER TWICE THE LENGTH OF THE BOARD'S PERIMETER
FOR THE DRAWSTRING * ORIGINAL PADDED COVER OR
SEVERAL LAYERS OF BLANKET FOR PADDING

Ironing board cover

*You can spend a long time in very close proximity
to an ironing board every week. And for the rest
of the time, the surfboard of the laundry world
has to perch somewhere, often in view, so there
are two good reasons why your ironing board
should be beautiful as well as functional.*

1. Remove any worn or old covers that are not in good
condition from the board. However, if your existing cover
is fine, you can use this as your padding for the new cover.

2. Lay the fabric on a large table or on a clean sheet on the
floor with the right side facing down. Place the ironing
board face down onto it and draw a chalk line around the
perimeter of the board about 10cm from the edge. Cut out
the shape. Now fold over a 2cm hem all around the edge,
pin it and iron the hem in place.

3. Starting at the pointier end of the board, sew the hem
to create a channel that is at least 1cm wide for the
drawstring to pass through, removing the pins as you
go. Leave a small gap of about 5cm between the start
and end of the stitching to allow you to feed the
drawstring into and out of the hem.

4. Attach the safety pin to one end of your strong string
or tape and pass the pin through the channel around the
perimeter of the cover, feeding the drawstring through
with it. Push it out through the other end of the hem.

5. Cut several layers of blanket to the size and shape
of the ironing board plus a couple of centimetres on
all sides. Stack these on top of the board to create a
thick layer of padding or use the old cover as padding.
Now place the new cover over the top.

6. Pulling on both ends of the drawstring, gradually tighten
the cover over the board. Keep pulling until the hemmed
edge is as tight as it can be under the board, then tie the
string securely in place.

YOU WILL NEED:

....

1 TABLESPOON VODKA * CLEAN LAUNDRY SPRAY
BOTTLE OF AROUND 500ML * ESSENTIAL OIL, SUCH
AS LAVENDER OR ROSE * 450ML DISTILLED WATER

Linen water

There is a long and complicated way of distilling flower water using ice, pots and hot stoves. This is a simple method that makes all your ironing smell delicious. Traditionally, rose and lavender have been used for making linen waters, so I've suggested those for this project, but you can experiment to see which essential oils you like best. If you are about to use the resulting linen water on your finest silk shirt, test a little area before you wade in to ensure that it does not mark the fabric. Use up the linen water within one month of making.

1. Place the vodka in the spray bottle, add up to a teaspoon of essential oil and shake well.

2. Add the distilled water and shake again. The contents may go a little cloudy, but that is fine.

3. Label the bottle - ensuring that you add the date of making. Spritz over sheets and clothing before ironing for a fresh, sweet scent, shaking well before each use.

Box files four ways

Storage boxes and files look lovely covered in fabric and paper you can use wrapping paper, ends of rolls of wallpaper, fabric remnants left over from decorating schemes or any paper ephemera.

If you are covering lots of files in large sheets of paper or fabric, make a template to speed up the process.

You can line the files too if you like, by patchworking little pieces of papers or fabric all around the inside and letting it dry before you begin covering the outside. Work the scraps around any fitting the file has for a neat finish.

If you are using box files or containers, cover the ends of the files with their own strip of material and then wrap a long strip of paper or fabric around the flap, sides and base.

FOR FILES COVERED IN LARGE PIECES OF PAPER, MAPS OR FABRIC

1. To make a template for files of the same size, open out a file onto a large sheet of newspaper and draw around the outline. Add 2–3cm to all edges and use a pencil and ruler to mark the cutting line. Cut out this template. Now place the open file onto it. Mark the top and bottom of the spine on the template and cut down towards this from the edge of the paper to make a little tongue to tuck inside when the file is covered. Cut off the corners of the template at 45 degrees, just up to the pencil line, so that there is a mitred effect once the paper or fabric is folded around a file.

2. Check that the template fits your files, then place it on the paper or fabric and draw around it using pencil or chalk. Cut out the shape, then lay it out flat with the right side facing down.

3. Brush glue lightly all over the outside of the file and lay it in the centre of the covering. Gently smooth the fabric or paper in place over the file, and then leave it to dry for half an hour or so. Now add a little glue to the 2–3cm of paper or fabric intended to be stuck inside the file and smooth the fabric or paper in place, including the tongue. Open and close the files a couple of times to ensure the covering is not too tight and leave it open to allow the whole thing to dry.

4. Glue buttons and ribbon in place if you would like to create a mock fastening and line the interior, if you wish, with contrasting fabric or paper, using the same technique.

FOR STAMPS OR SCRAPS OF PAPER

You can cover the files in a patchwork of smaller pieces of paper and ephemera or stamps. Try pages from books, old manuscripts, newspapers or scraps of fabric. Cover a little area of the file in a thin layer of PVA glue and add the pieces one at a time. Keep adding the scraps until the whole area is covered. Don't worry if some of the surface of the pieces have glue on them, you can cover the whole piece in a coat at the end for a more durable surface.

Cutlery basket

Vintage cutlery is very pretty - odd knives and forks, not quite as shiny as they should be, cute teaspoons, bone handles and ornate scrolls, monograms and makers' marks. You can often pick up lovely pieces at fairs and thrift shops, but rarely will you find a full set or even more than a couple of matching pieces, so you have to pick and choose your way through what is on offer.

There are traditional styles with pattern names such as King's, Rattail, Bead and my favourite, Fiddle. You might like to select a favourite pattern and build up your collection slowly, or enjoy an eclectic mix of different styles of vintage cutlery. Half a dozen pieces of good silver plate cutlery still regularly cost the price of a cup of coffee and rarely, amongst the makers' marks and symbols and the grades of plate marked on the reverse of spoons and forks, you might find a little lion lurking, the sign of solid silver. You should expect to pay a whole lot more for one of these, unless it is your lucky day.

What to do with your growing collection of knives and forks is less of a problem if you have a fitted kitchen full of drawers. However, in our pared-back, freestanding state, a cutlery basket seemed like a good idea.

1. Place the pots inside the basket, fitting larger and smaller ones next to each other until you have enough pots for types of cutlery.

2. Pop all the teaspoons in a small glass or pot, children's forks in another and so on, placing your cheese knives, serving spoons and knives and forks in individual pots until everything is neatly arranged in its own space.

SQUARE OF BLANKET, TICKING OR UPHOLSTERY FABRIC OR
EVEN AN OLD TABLECLOTH * SEWING MACHINE * COTTON
* PINKING SHEARS * CORD OR RIBBON, JUST OVER FOUR TIMES
THE LENGTH OF ONE EDGE * LARGE SAFETY PIN * GLASS TO
DRAW AROUND * TAILOR'S CHALK * SEWING NEEDLE * PINS
* IRON * EXTRA FABRIC FOR LINING IF REQUIRED

Blanket storage bag

This is a simple drawstring bag that spreads out totally to make a flat playing, packing or even eating surface. You can choose your fabric and cord to suit the use. Ticking fabric and rope is perfect for the beach. A pretty embroidered tablecloth and ribbon for the back of the bathroom door or a big blanket and woven tape for playing Lego.

1. Cut out a square of fabric using pinking shears just larger than the size you want your mat to be. (If you are using a tablecloth that is already hemmed then ignore this stage.)

2. Lay the fabric out good side down, fold in half and mark the middle of each side with tailor's chalk.

3. Use your glass as a template to draw a semicircle at the edge of each halfway point, and also as a guide to mark a quarter circle at each corner.

4. Use pinking sheers to cut around the circles. Turn over the pinked edges towards the middle, pin and press in place so once again you are left with a square.

5. Sew along just inside the pinked edges making sure you leave a big enough channel to fit the safety pin and ribbon through easily. When you get to a semicircle, sew straight across so you leave an opening for the drawstring. Remove the pins.

6. Tie off any loose ends then attach the safety pin to the end of the cord. Push the pin through the channel at the edge of the square and move it all the way round leaving a trail of cord in the channel.

7. Stretch the fabric out completely flat then overlap the end of the ribbon or cord and sew it firmly together by hand or using a sewing machine.

8. To pull into a bag, gather up all eight of the bits of cord that you can see and pull until the fabric gathers evenly and the swag is safely inside.

Remember that the cords or ribbons may be a hazard to very little children.

TIP If you would like to add a lining fabric, cut a square with pinking shears that will fit just inside the area made by the circles. Pin it in place then turn the edges over onto it and when you sew down the edges you will also attach the lining.

CHILD'S PLAY

YOU WILL NEED:
....
COUNTERS FOR AS MANY ROWS AS YOU NEED ∗ HAND-
HELD DRILL AND SMALL DRILL BIT ∗ TAPE MEASURE
∗ FLEXIBLE GARDEN WIRE ∗ SCISSORS OR PLIERS
SUITABLE FOR CUTTING WIRE ∗ HEAVY DUTY STAPLE
GUN, OR U-SHAPED NAILS AND SMALL HAMMER
∗ PICTURE FRAME WITH HANGING ATTACHMENT

Abacus

You have got to love an abacus. Right from a really early age our children could understand the correlation between the brightly coloured counters, chocolate buttons and tidy bedrooms. Who would have thought that so much leverage could be gained by simply moving a bead along a wire?

There are heaps of modern and ancient examples to be found out there and, even if you are not using them to explain about tens and units, they make for good decorative pieces in small people's rooms.

If you want to make your own abacus, don't be held back by thinking that you have to use only beads for counters. Collect seashells, small cars, driftwood, cotton reels or anything with a hole in it to thread onto your frame. Or if you find suitably sized but hole-less objects, you can make the holes yourself using a hand-held drill and a small drill bit.

1. Get all your counters in a line and decide on the look you wish to create for your abacus. Consider how many lines would fit well into your picture frame.

2. Use a hand-held drill to make holes very carefully in any of the objects that do not have a natural path to thread the wire or string through. Ensure that you drill through a spot on each counter that allows it to balance nicely when you have threaded it onto the wire.

3. Measure the lengths of wire you need for each row, adding 10cm to each length, then cut the number of lines you will need for your picture frame. Thread the objects onto the wires and make a loop at each end.

4. Staple or nail each wire carefully in place on the back of the frame. Make sure that the part of the frame to which you are attaching the wire is wider than the length of the staples or nails, so that they will not be visible from the front.

5. Depending on the depth of the counters that you have used, you may need to add some spacers to the back of the frame so everything moves easily along the wires when the frame is hanging on the wall. Position a halved cork in each corner of the back of your frame and nail them to the frame before hanging it on the wall.

Mobile

There are heaps of modern gadgets for children today, but a good old-fashioned mobile still does the trick and looks pretty in a nursery or strung from a tree in the garden.

You can make mobiles out of coat hangers or wooden dowling, but this version uses a florist's ring for a wreath and flexible fine garden wire.

Make sure you don't add trinkets that are too heavy and that everything is securely attached and well out of the reach of children.

Like the abacuses you can also drill holes in any wooden toys and run the wire through the hole created.

1. Arrange your toys and trinkets in a circle roughly the same size as your wreath ring.

2. Snip a length of wire slightly longer than the hanging length that you want.

3. Wind it around the body of your animal, toy or trinket or thread it through any holes it may have. Twist the wire several times and trim off the excess short end.

4. Halfway up the wire, wrap it several times around a pencil to create a mini spring effect and then fasten the other end to the wreath ring. Do this by wrapping the wire around the ring several times and then snipping off any loose ends.

5. Lay the wreath ring out flat on the table, with the attached wires radiating from it, and add the rest of the toys.

6. Add a length of wire to make a hanging loop, attaching it by winding it several times around the wire ring.

TIP I have used lead farm animals here, but choose toys that are suitable for the age of your child, and make sure that they are kept well out of reach of any babies or small children.

Dolls' houses

It is always useful if a piece of furniture can be used in a couple of ways and these shelves are perfect for small spaces and are easily converted back into a shelf, if necessary. You could decorate the entire unit or just one shelf. And there's no need to stick to a traditional doll's house theme – make your shelves into a zoo, farmyard or any play scene that your kids will love. You can add lots of detail and interior features, or simply arrange dolls' house furniture on one shelf.

1. Make a plan for your shelves. Choose your theme and decide if you will apply it to the entire unit or just the shelf that is the most easily accessible to children. If the shelves are not new, check them all over to ensure that there are no nails or bits of splintered wood that might hurt small fingers. See page 20 for tips on restoring and painting wood and ensure the entire unit is suitably finished before decorating the shelves.

2. To wallpaper a shelf, measure the length and height of the two sides and the back of the shelf and cut a strip of paper to size. Measure the 'floor', too, and cut a strip of paper or an offcut of carpet to size. A craft knife is best for cutting through thick carpet, but ensure that you have a suitable cutting mat or board beneath. Alternatively, paint the interior of each shelf a different colour to represent the rooms.

3. When you have cut all the paper and carpet to size and painted any shelf interiors, stick the paper and carpet in place. Spread a thin layer of PVA glue over each surface you want to cover, then smooth the paper in place. It may look a little crinkly if you have areas of thick glue, but they normally look better after the glue has dried.

4. Glue the carpet or pretend grass in place or secure it using double-sided tape.

5. When you have each interior finished, add decorations. Tiny picture frames hanging from little tacks or drawing pins look good. Paint or stick on squares of paper for windows and doors and add interior details such as door frames and window frames with thick marker pens and a ruler. If you are making a garden scene, use more glue to add cut-out trees, gates and fences to the backgrounds. Arrange your furniture in each layer then present your house to its new owner.

YOU WILL NEED:

TAPE MEASURE * PAPER, PENCIL AND PAPER SCISSORS FOR THE TEMPLATE * SIX PANELS OF UPHOLSTERY-WEIGHT FABRIC (THE SIZE OF THE BEANBAG IS UP TO YOU - THEY CAN BE SQUARE OR RECTANGULAR AND FROM 50CM SQUARE FOR A CHILD'S SIZE) * TAILOR'S CHALK OR FABRIC MARKER * FABRIC SCISSORS * SIX PANELS OF LINING * FABRIC THE SAME SIZE AS ABOVE (AN OLD SHEET OR ANY RECLAIMED FABRIC IS FINE) * PINS * SEWING MACHINE * SEWING THREAD * IRON * POLYSTYRENE BEADS TO FILL BAG OR OLD BEANBAG TO RECLAIM BEANS * HAND-SEWING NEEDLE (OPTIONAL) * VELCRO STRIPS THE SAME WIDTH AS THE BEANBAG

Beanbags

The more time I spend doing children's activities, the more time I seem to spend on the floor. These simple beanbag cubes make the whole process of child's play a little more comfortable, if you can wrestle the dog, the cat and the children off them first. They also offer a great way of using up smaller pieces of fabric and you could make parts of the cushion out of simple patchwork panels too. Make the bottom panel out of a hard-wearing fabric so it can withstand wear and tear. If you would like a handle, stitch a short length of ribbon into one of the seams. (Although, be warned - this makes it very tempting to transform a lovely seat into a pillow-fighting weapon!)

1. Choose the size of your beanbag, then make a template for each different shaped face – remember to incorporate your chosen seam allowance. For a square you will need one template with sides that measure the same or, for a rectangular beanbag, first draw the template for the top and bottom panels, then use the measurements for the long and short edges to help you create the other two pieces of your pattern.

2. Place your fabrics on a table with the right sides down and draw around the pattern pieces using chalk or a fabric marker. Cut out each panel, apart from the one for the base. For this, add 5cm to each of the longer edges to allow for the hem and opening. Cut out this larger panel too. Repeat the entire process on the lining fabric, but without allowing the extra 5cm on the base panel.

3. First, make the lining. Pin the panels together with right sides facing to make a cube. Using your sewing machine, sew along all but one of the edges, removing the pins as you go. Turn the fabric so the right sides are out, pushing out the corners into a cube shape. Turn in a hem that is the width of your seam allowance on both sides of the open edge and iron it in place.

4. Carefully pour the polystyrene beads into the cube until it is nearly full, then pin together the turned-in hems. Machine or hand-sew the opening securely closed.

5. To make the outer cube, first lay out the panel with the extra 5cm, longest side towards you and fold and then cut it in half widthways. Turn over a hem of about 1cm on this newly cut edge and iron it flat to make a hemmed opening. Sew it in place using the sewing machine. Position the velcro strips on the bottom of one piece and the top of the other so when they attach you have created a panel the same size as the other five. Sew them in place using a sewing machine.

6. Repeat the pinning and sewing process but this time, sew all of the seams of your cube. Open the velcro and turn the cube fabric so the right sides are facing out. Feed in the bean bag and secure the cover shut with the velcro.

TIP If you would like to add letters or numbers to your cube, appliqué these onto the fabric before you begin the sewing-up process. Choose a contrasting fabric and apply a piece of iron-on interfacing to the back. Draw on your chosen letter, number or shape and cut it out. Position it on the fabric panel, pin it, then zigzag, straight stitch or blanket stitch it on. Make sure that you have it the right way up when you make up the rest of the project!

YOU WILL NEED:

NEWSPAPER OR LARGE SHEETS OF PLAIN PAPER * PENCIL * PAPER
SCISSORS OR CRAFT KNIFE AND CUTTING MAT * WALLPAPER
* PERMANENT MARKERS * STICKY TACK * TUBE OF STRONG
WALLPAPER PASTE AND BRUSH * EXTRA STRONG DIY FIXATIVE
* SMALL TOYS, CARS, FIGURES, TRINKETS, SHELLS, BUTTONS OR
BEADS * POSTER OR EMULSION PAINTS * SOFT, CLEAN ERASER

Ceiling and wall installations

While I was still at school, I persuaded my long-suffering parents that a wall in my bedroom would look great modelled on one of Monet's amazing water lily paintings. It took ages to complete and I think I ended up actually staple gunning strips of fabric to the wall when my parents were out of the house. The result was impressive, if just for its sheer scale, but the installation was very difficult to dust - and a lesson in the art of decorating was experienced early on in life. Having learned from my mistakes, I would advise you to keep your own designs bold and simple and don't glue anything too precious or difficult to dust in place. Choose your patterns, toys and trinkets with your child's tastes in mind.

Ceiling designs are great above cots to keep babies interested, but make doubly sure that anything attached is glued very firmly in place.

There are some simply amazing adhesive products available if you would like to attach real toys to a wall, or find a type tray to fill with trinkets for an updatable option. A ceiling installation is not for the fainthearted - you need to have something stable to stand on that elevates you to the height you need to reach. Alternatively, keep your feet firmly on the ground and opt for a wall installation.

1. Make a plan for your installation. The following ideas are intended to get your imagination started:

- farm, fields, fences and trees with attached animals

- villages with little wooden houses

- streets and roads with cars

- train tracks, stations and trains

- abstract patterns with buttons and beads

- grassy meadows with flowers and butterflies

- palaces, castles and soldiers.

2. Once you are happy with your plan, start to make the background elements out of cut-out pieces of wallpaper. First, draw the shapes on newspaper or plain paper and cut them out to use as templates to draw around on the back of the wallpaper. Alternatively, draw them freehand onto the back of the wallpaper. When positioning your shapes on the wallpaper, check that you are using any appropriate areas of the wallpaper's pattern if there are any that will look good in your scheme. Cut out the designs carefully. Add any details to the wallpaper shapes with markers at this point. Use sticky tack to position the shapes temporarily on the walls or ceiling.

3. Now add wallpaper tracks and roads, fences or little characters and stick those in place too. Keep layering up your shapes until you have a satisfying design. Sit on the floor to check your design looks good from down there too. For small installations, make a wallpaper frame or fence to go around the outside of the design.

4. When you have made all of your wallpaper shapes, lightly mark around the outside of each piece on the wall in fine pencil, then remove all of the shapes.

5. Apply paste to the back of each wallpaper shape, then position it in its correct place, using the pencil outlines to guide you, smoothing out any creases and wiping away excess glue.

6. To attach real toys, squeeze on a small amount of super-strong fixative to the flattest area of each item you wish to attach to the wall and press the object firmly in place until set (this will not take long).

7. Add any fine details to your design with poster or emulsion paints or use a thick marker pen. Stalks of flowers, tracks for trains, fences for fields and doors can be easily picked out this way. When everything is totally dry, use a soft, clean eraser to remove any visible fine pencil lines.

YOU WILL NEED:

WALLPAPER * STAMPS * INK PADS OR ACRYLIC PAINT
* A SMALL SQUARE OF BLANKET OR FELT FABRIC
TO MAKE A PAD * YOU MIGHT NEED: RULER * TAPE
MEASURE * COMPASSES * PENCIL

Printing your own wallpaper

Lots of pattern and colour are common themes in the decoration of vintage homes and using stamps to include a little personal touch to wallpaper only adds to the layers and interest on the walls. Neither stamps nor wallpaper have to be vintage pieces for this project, but mixing in some old-fashioned elements will make the finished wallpaper sit well on the walls of any house that has a nostalgic feel.

You can buy plain or very subtly patterned paper and add your own motifs or letters across it in a geometric pattern, or you can go totally freestyle with handprints and prints of little feet, or find some boldly patterned paper to add your own special something. Once you have done your printing, you'll need to be aware of the basic principles of hanging wallpaper, so see page 19 for the simple guide to papering.

WHICH PAPER?

Whichever paper you choose, test that your stamps or drawings will print onto it and dry properly, as some special papers are coated and will not take further printing. Also, check that the surface is smooth so that all of the detail of the stamp is picked up. However, the aim of this project is not to produce complicated intricate patterns, but to add a little frivolity to the walls.

For the ultimate personal touch, bear in mind that there are companies who will create a rubber stamp for you out of pretty much any image you send to them, and will have your finished stamp drop on your doormat the morning after you have sent in your design (see page 188).

WORKING ON PLAIN PAPER

Plan your design on a small piece of the roll. Use a ruler, tape measure or compass and tiny pencil crosses to mark out where to place your stamps and build up the design and colours on this piece as a guide to work from. Be realistic about how much time it will take to repeat this design around a whole room's worth of paper and remember that, sometimes, less is more.

When it comes to choosing stamps for plain paper, the world is your oyster. The following suggestions are intended to get your imagination rolling:

- initials or monograms
- a child's simple line drawings made into stamps
- basic heart, spot, square or flower shapes
- leaves
- handprint or footprint stamps, or the real thing.

WORKING ON PATTERNED PAPER

Add little quirky stamps to fancy printed papers. Use the existing pattern on the paper as a guide for where to place your stamps, then print away amongst the roses, toile or trellis.

When choosing stamps for patterned paper, the following suggestions for stamp designs often work well over patterns:

- bees and butterflies
- insects and beetles
- messages or names
- dogs and cats or paw prints
- flowers.

1. Roll out a stretch of the paper on a smooth surface such as a big table or a newspaper-covered expanse of floor. Weigh down the paper if it wants to roll back up - use a book or two.

2. Stamp or draw away according to your design, cleaning the stamps between colours. Work your way along the unrolled section of paper.

3. Wait until the ink is dry, then roll up the printed stretch of paper and continue printing another section. If it takes too long to dry, have two rolls on the go at once. Keep going until you have enough printed wallpaper for your panel, wall or room.

YOU WILL NEED:

WALKING STICK * PAPER, PENCIL AND PAPER SCISSORS FOR THE TEMPLATE * TAILOR'S CHALK * BROWN FELT, JUMPER OR BLANKET FABRIC * FABRIC SCISSORS * SCRAPS OF FELT, FABRIC OR BLANKET FOR EARS, EYES AND FACE DETAILS * PINS * SEWING MACHINE * SEWING THREAD * POLYESTER OR SHEEP'S WOOL STUFFING * HAND-SEWING NEEDLE * STRONG THREAD * HOT GLUE GUN OR FABRIC GLUE * WOOL OR FRINGING FROM AN OLD BLANKET OR RUG * RIBBON OR OLD BELTS TO MAKE THE HARNESS * OPTIONAL: ACRYLIC OR CHALK PAINT * PAINTBRUSH * CASTER FROM OLD FURNITURE

Walking stick hobby horse

The last-minute discovery of the fact that the party our daughter was about to attend one afternoon was a mock gymkhana saw the first walking stick hobby horse emerge from our stable. Most thrift shops have an umbrella stand tucked into a corner in which you'll find a couple of walking sticks, some old golf clubs and an umbrella or two. This project makes great use of the walking sticks.

1. First, make the base of the head. Wash and scrub the walking stick really well, leave it to dry then give the whole thing a coat of paint if you wish. See page 20 for guidelines on painting. The curved top of the walking stick makes a perfect support for the horse's head but, as these differ from one walking stick to the next, check that the top of your walking stick fits within the outline of your horse's head and adjust to fit.

2. Draw out a simple horse head shape onto newspaper and cut it to make a template. Lay the largest template onto the wrong side of your main piece of fabric with the head facing to the left and chalk the outline. Then flip the template so that the head faces to the right and chalk the outline so that you have pieces for each side of the horse's head. Cut out both pieces. Now cut out a pair of ears, twice on the main fabric and twice on a contrast-coloured scrap and cut out the ear pieces. You can mix and match the colours to create your own favourite nag.

3. Pin together the two head pieces with the right sides facing and, with a 2cm seam allowance, sew around the entire head using a sewing machine, removing the pins as you go and leaving the neck open for stuffing. Check that all the pins are removed then turn the fabric for the head piece so that the right sides face outwards.

4. Pin together the ear pieces with their right sides facing and sew around the outside edges of both, leaving the bottom edge open. Remove the pins and turn the ears so that the right sides of the fabric face outwards. Stuff the ears with a little of your chosen stuffing and hand-sew the bottom closed, then pleat the base of the ears and sew through all the layers to give the ears some shape.

5. Cut two slits into the top of the horse's head where the ears look best. Pop the base of the ears through the slit, then sew them tightly in place all through the layers of fabric.

6. Begin to stuff the horse's head, packing the stuffing tightly into the nose area. Place the head onto the handle end of the walking stick and continue to stuff the whole head. Use a long piece of strong thread, doubled and knotted at the end, and hand-sew a running stitch all around the bottom of the neck. Apply plenty of fabric glue or use a glue gun to stick the fabric to the walking stick, drawing the thread together to gather the neck tightly around the walking stick.

7. When the glue has dried, begin to add detail to your horse. Cut out eyes, nostrils, a muzzle and a lower lip, then sew or glue them in place. You can add face details, such as little teeth and wool eyelashes, if you want.

8. If you have any fringing from an old blanket, use this to make the mane, sewing it in place between the ears and down along the neck. If you are using wool, lay the threads across the neck and sew them in place, then add a little forelock with some longer threads.

9. To make a rein for your pony, use a loop of ribbon or an old belt and sew it in place under the neck of the horse.

10. Finally, if you have managed to scavenge a caster, screw it in place on the bottom of the stick.

Chest of drawers four ways

An essential piece of furniture for children's rooms. Simple to update as they grow, a chest of drawers is an easy piece to make your own.

This, probably French, chest was in good condition when I bought it at an antiques market but they turn up in all sizes and shapes in varying condition at boot sales to antique shops.

When shopping for a chest of drawers it's a good idea to take a tape measure and have an idea of the size of piece you are after. Take a look at the back and underside if you can to make sure that it is sound. Make sure that older pieces are still substantial enough for general use, and that woodworm or rot has not made them too weak. Use a liberal dose of woodworm treatment if you suspect that the piece is still under attack.

If drawers are difficult to open check that they are in the right slots by swapping their position around. Or remove the drawers and rub the runners with a plain candle to ease the opening and shutting.

Squatter, fatter versions might be more suitable for children's rooms as tall versions, laden with clothing, have been known to tip forward if all the drawers are open at once.

SHIP-SHAPE

This is a super speedy way to change the look of your drawers. Carefully measure and cut panels of paper to fit each drawer front. Unscrew the handles and snip out small shapes for any escutcheons or keyholes before pasting the drawer front with a fine coat of PVA glue. Smooth the paper in place and when it is dry, refix the handles in place. For a sealed surface you can also paint over the paper with another coat of PVA glue.

FANTASTIC FLORALS

Flowers cut from you favourite fine cotton fabric can also be stuck to the drawer fronts. Carefully snip around pretty scraps until you have enough flowers and paste them in place with PVA glue.

BRIGHT AND BEAUTIFUL

Pink and white chalk paints, scraped and sanded to make a old painted look, can cover up a multitude of sins if your drawers have seen better days. Use layers of different paint and light and dark wax to achieve the look you are after.

SIMPLE CHIC

Painted and waxed with neat edging to each drawer, this completes the journey of this piece of furniture from nursery to first flat. Paint all over in your base colour and wait until totally dry and then mask around the borders of each drawer or edge and paint with a contrasting colour. When completely dry remove the masking tape and wax the whole piece with soft, clear wax.

DECORATION

YOU WILL NEED:
....
SUITABLE FRAME WITH WOODEN PANEL OR GLASS
PANE * CHALK PAINT(S) * PAINTBRUSH * TACKS OR
GLUE GUN AND TAPE TO SECURE PANEL OR GLASS
PANE * CORD AND ATTACHMENTS TO HANG FRAME
* COLOURED CHALKS TO DECORATE YOUR BLACKBOARD

Blackboards

I like pretty much everything about a blackboard, apart from the black bit. They are always where you left them, great for saving paper and refreshingly low tech. And now, with a palette of pretty chalk paints available, you can have a board in French grey, garden green or Aegean blue. Teemed up with coloured chalks and an old frame, this vintage schoolroom staple suddenly reminds you a whole lot less of algebra.

You can try using one large frame, or several together for each member of the family or days of the week. And you might like to pick another chalk-paint colour to add permanent words or symbols to your board.

It is worth spending a bit of time looking for the easiest sort of frame to convert. The perfect one will have a good-looking border that you can leave as it is or paint, and a smooth wooden panel on the back to use as your board. If you find a frame that you love without a panel you will need to have a piece of MDF or wood cut to size. You can also apply chalk paint directly onto glass, but over time it may scratch off, so you'll need another coat.

1. Start by preparing the frame. Remove any pictures, tacks or tape from the back and brush away any loose dust or paint. Be particularly careful if handling frames with glass as the edges of the glass may be chipped and sharp. Keep any reusable fixings.

2. Prepare the backing board in the same way as you did the frame in step 1 and dust it well before painting. Have a look at the painting section (page 20), then paint the board. Apply two or three thick coats of paint, allowing each coat to dry before applying the next. You can layer up different colours and distress the edges of the board for a more knocked-back look and use a different coloured paint to add details, names or words.

3. Paint your frame. Allow both the frame and the painted board to dry. Add the attachments to hang the frame if neccesary.

4. Pop the board into the frame and secure it in place. You can do this by gluing the glass or board to the frame with a glue gun, using any fixings that you salvaged or by tacking it in place. Finally, add a thick border of tape across all the joins on the back and hang in place.

YOU WILL NEED:

SELECTION OF VINTAGE PAPERS * SCISSORS OR CRAFT KNIFE,
BOARD AND METAL RULE * TAPE MEASURE * PVA GLUE AND BRUSH
* PAPER FOR TEMPLATE * CLEAR ACRYLIC VARNISH (OPTIONAL)

Updating stairs

If you have a wooden staircase this is a really pretty option. I removed the old worn carpets from our stairs and chose a selection of vintage papers to cover each riser. I sanded the bare wood and then used masking tape to mark out the lines up each side before painting. A couple of coats of acrylic paint makes the sides easy to sweep down, and the area where all the wear is in the middle stays matt and unslippery.

1. Measure one of the step risers in the middle of the stairs and use the dimensions to create a paper template. Check that this fits on all the steps. The first and last often vary slightly.

2. Use the template to draw around on the back of your wallpapers. Cut out the pieces using scissors or a craft knife on a suitable cutting surface. If any steps measured different sizes then cut out the paper to fit these too.

3. Arrange the papers so that they look good together if you are using more than one and then begin the sticking process.

4. Make sure the stairs are free of dust and any loose particles and then paint one riser at a time with a thin layer of PVA glue and smooth the paper in place. Push out any air bubbles or creases towards the edge of the stairs and pay particular attention to the edges so that they are well glued in place.

5. Wait until the glue is totally dry, about 24 hours, and then cover the surface of each riser with a fine coat of PVA glue or clear acrylic varnish to protect the papers. You will have a more matt finish if you use the varnish.

YOU WILL NEED:

TAPE MEASURE * BLANKET * TAILOR'S CHALK * EGG CUP, GLASS
OR PLATE TO USE AS A TEMPLATE FOR THE SCALLOPS (OPTIONAL)
* FABRIC SCISSORS * HOLE PUNCH * E-SHAPED CURTAIN HOOKS
* TRIMMINGS (OPTIONAL) * SEWING MACHINE (OPTIONAL)
* SEWING THREAD (OPTIONAL)

Blanket curtain

This is a super simple, cheat-like-mad option for making a warm curtain in a hurry that is cheap, effective and great for keeping draughts and winter chills at bay. There are many ways of fixing curtains, but this one uses simple e-shaped hooks and a track, which is often found in place when you move into a new house, the previous owners having left with their favourite curtains. The blanket will need to be a substantial warm one rather than a floaty mohair throw in order for the fabric to have enough strength to support the weight of the curtain where the hooks go through it.

If you don't have a curtain track in place, in front of a door perhaps, you can also use a piece of strong herringbone tape, threaded through the holes and then attached with hooks, to make a warm, draught excluding curtain for winter.

For a traditional pair of curtains, cut the blanket in half and scallop down the edges as well as the bottom. Or just go for one large curtain. This was originally used as a temporary solution to cover an old and draughty window in my workroom, but three years on, it still hangs beautifully.

If the idea of cutting into the fabric does not appeal, curtain clips are available with super snappy crocodile teeth that clasp the fabric tightly. These can be used on any fabric, but for weight versions like this blanket you will have to make sure that you use plenty of clips across the width of the curtain to weight it evenly. These can be threaded onto a curtain pole and mean you can make instant curtains without cutting into any precious material.

When summer comes, you can make light and airy versions out of crisp vintage sheets, tablecloths or pretty fabrics.

1. Measure the width of your window and the length from the hooks to the point at which you want the bottom of the curtain to sit. You can use one whole swathe of blanket to cover the window or cut it in half to make a pair of curtains. If you want your curtain to have some gathers, the blanket can be up to twice the width of the window.

2. Give the blanket a good hot wash with plenty of washing powder to slightly felt and therefore tighten up the fabric. If the blanket has pretty stitching or a nice edging, use this edge along the top of the curtain.

3. To trim the blanket to the length you require, make a chalk line all the way across the width, then mark scallop shapes below this line by drawing around an egg cup, glass or plate, depending on the size of the scallop you prefer. Cut around the scallops with sharp scissors.

4. Use a hole punch along the top edge of the curtain to make tiny holes arranged 10–15cm apart and at least 2cm in from the top edge of the fabric. Slip the curtain hooks through the holes and into place on the track for a quick and effective curtain. To add detail, stitch lengths of lace or ribbons down the leading edge of the curtain or to disguise the line of hooks, if they are visible at the top.

YOU WILL NEED:
....
PAINTBRUSHES • ROLLERS • ROLLER TRAYS
• MASKING TAPE • CONTRASTING PAINTS
• TAPE MEASURE • CHALK • TEMPLATES FOR
ANY EDGES • CLEAR WAX TO SEAL FLOOR

Painted floors

I would rather have a rickety set of painted floorboards than a carpet. They don't need to be only one colour either as you can paint pretty edges, pretend tiles and imaginary mats about the place and have an easy-to-brush, scrub or paint over solution.

I just love the vintage finish that you can create using the chalk paint. For the floor effects mentioned above, masking tape and a selection of brushes and small rollers are helpful to prevent having to clean kit all the time.

FOR A TILED FLOOR

1. Make sure that the whole floor is totally clean and dry and dust-free. Mask any skirting boards, fittings or pipes for a really smart finish and then begin to paint. Follow the instructions on your chosen paint carefully and paint the whole floor in the lighter colour first then wait a couple of days for a really dry finish.

2. Measure and chalk on the lines of any tiles across the floor. You can choose to place them conventionally in line with the walls, or at a 90 degree-angle for a diamond pattern or you can simply mask on 'grouting' to look like old castle floors.

3. Choose masking tape that is suitable for the newly painted floor and then tape along the edges of the background tiles until you have covered the whole area of the floor. Leave a border all around the edge that follows all of the indents in the wall if you wish. As I like a particularly quick and effective process I often leave areas under baths or around sinks plain. If you want to be reminded which areas you need to paint, put a cross in the centre of all the masked areas that you are adding dark paint to. It is surprisingly easy to paint in the wrong place when you are engrossed in getting the best finish. When the masking is complete, paint your way out of the room and leave everything to dry completely.

4. When you are totally convinced that the floor is dry in all areas, peel off the masking tape and survey the results.

FOR A SCALLOPED BORDER

If you want to add any pattern to your borders, you can add scallops freehand, or make a template by drawing round a glass or plate with chalk and then painting inside the lines.

FOR MATS

Add mats in the same way by measuring, chalking and masking rectangles and painting inside to create the place to place your mat. You can make them simple one colour panels or add colour and pattern if you wish.

WAXING

All floors need to be finished with a layer of clear wax. Brush or rub over the surface with a soft cloth and then buff when set.

IMAGES OF YOUR CHOSEN SHAPES, TRACING PAPER, PENCIL AND
CARD, TO MAKE TEMPLATES OR PAPER PUNCHES OF YOUR CHOSEN
SHAPE * RUBBER STAMPS AND INK AND/OR PENS (OPTIONAL)
* PAPER EPHEMERA * PAPER SCISSORS * RECLAIMED PICTURE
FRAME WITH BACKING PANEL OR STRETCHED CANVAS * THICK
CARTRIDGE PAPER (IF USING A RECLAIMED PICTURE FRAME)
* RULER * SOFT ERASER * INSTANT ADHESIVE OR DOUBLE-SIDED
STICKY PADS * TAPE (IF USING A RECLAIMED PICTURE FRAME)

Butterfly pictures

*Simple, yet highly effective, these pictures
and displays made of cut-out pieces of paper
make wonderful gifts and cards for weddings,
christenings and birthdays, as you can make
a personalised picture to match any theme.
For the paper, you could cut up old maps (of
places significant to the recipient, perhaps),
wallpaper, coloured papers, music scores,
or hand paint or draw, say, butterflies from
a nature book, and cut out your drawings.
Your shapes can be cut freehand, or first drawn
in pencil, but if cutting out seems like a chore
to you, paper punches come in many shapes
and sizes, making the job the work of a moment.
Stick your cut-outs onto a sheet of card to put
into a reclaimed glassless frame, or stick them
directly onto a stretched canvas. You could
add names and dates to your picture, by hand
or with rubber stamps.*

1. Plan your design before you begin. One simple shape
(such as a heart, star or butterfly) cut out many times can
look great. If you are not using a paper punch, you could
print out a shape on paper or card or find one in a book
and trace it onto card to obtain the outline of the shape you
want. If you are adding text, practise stamping or writing it
so that you know how much space to leave in your design
for the text. Transfer the shape onto the back of your
papers as many times as you need to create your
cut outs. Cut or punch out the shapes.

2. If you are using a reclaimed frame, cut a piece of thick
cartridge paper to fit behind the edge of the frame so
that it is just a tiny bit smaller (a few millimetres) than
the backing panel. You will stick your shapes onto this.
Note how far from the edge of the paper you need to
position your shapes to ensure they do not become
squashed when you pop the finished work into the frame.

3. First, print names or dates onto the chosen spots on the
paper or canvas. Use a very faint pencil mark and rule a
line or two to help you make the letters straight and of the
same size, if it helps. When the ink is totally dry, gently rub
out the pencil marks with a soft, clean eraser.

4. Arrange the cut-out shapes onto the paper or canvas and
use a very faint pencil mark to note the position of each
one. Use instant adhesive or double-sided sticky pads to
stick the shapes in place. They can be stuck down flat, or
stuck down in one area and folded and raised from the
surface (this works well for butterfly wings, for instance).

5. If you are using a frame, pop the paper into the frame,
secure it shut and tape up the back for extra security,
if you like.

YOU WILL NEED:

TAPE MEASURE • SELECTION OF PAPERS THAT ARE STURDY
ENOUGH TO CUT AND PASTE • PENCIL OR CHALK • WALLPAPER
TABLE OR COVERED SURFACE FOR PASTING • PASTING BRUSH
• WALLPAPER PASTE, READY MIXED OR MADE UP ACCORDING
TO THE INSTRUCTIONS ON THE PACKET • CLEAN SOFT BRUSH
FOR SMOOTHING • WALLPAPER SCISSORS

Unusual wallpaper

The writing is on the wall ...or the scores, maps or postcards are. Wallpapering can be a daunting task. Before I begin I imagine long slippery rolls of precious paper covered in glue slithering away from me, and vast spaces that need to be covered. The reality is that even when taking your time to ensure that you get everything just right, wallpapering is really quite a speedy solution that gives the room an instant, exciting change. If you have not papered before, using small-scale pieces of paper, as in this project, can be an easy place to begin. Music scores, old atlases, pages from a book, even some newspaper all make effective wall coverings, but it is probably best to test a little of your chosen paper ephemera to ensure that it is up to the task before you begin.

1. Paste a small piece of paper onto a spare bit of wood or in the corner of the room to find out if the colours run and if you can achieve a suitable finish. For old maps and pages with crinkles, iron them before you begin, to remove some of the folds that have been created over time. For thicker papers or maps you might need to make up the paste so it is a little thicker than usual to hold them securely in place.

2. Measure the wall or walls that you are covering and roughly work out the area that you are looking to decorate.

Gather together enough papers to cover your chosen spot and make a plan for what will go where on the wall. You can make the pattern as contrived or free-flowing as you like. Measure and mark some gridlines onto the wall in pencil or chalk. A couple of vertical and horizontal lines will give you a guide if you have a good eye, or you might like to take a little more time and mark out a few more so that each row of papers has a line to follow.

3. Now begin the sticking process. Ensure that the walls are clean and dust free before you begin and always paste the paper and not the wall. Lay each piece of paper face down onto the gluing surface and brush over a thin, smooth covering of wallpaper paste.

4. Pop the paper into position on the wall, smoothing it carefully with the dry brush and working from the middle of the piece of paper to the edges to remove any bubbles or crinkles. Take the next piece and patchwork it beside the first, lining up the edges, either just overlapping the edges or placing it butted up to the last piece (for thin papers and irregular shapes, overlapping the edges is fine). Trim the pieces of paper to size around awkward corners or windows and keep sticking until you have covered the entire area. Smooth down each paper as you go, then once the whole lot is dry, paste back any corners of pieces that have become unstuck.

YOU WILL NEED:

SELECTION OF DIFFERENT PAPERS (FIVE OR MORE IS REALLY
EFFECTIVE) * GUILLOTINE OR CUTTING BOARD, CRAFT KNIFE
AND STEEL RULE * WALLPAPER PASTE, READY-MIXED OR MADE
UP TO THE INSTRUCTIONS ON THE PACKET * LARGE PASTING
BRUSH * LARGE SOFT BRUSH FOR SMOOTHING * PENCIL
* PLUMB LINE (WEIGHT ON A STRING) * CHALK * STEP LADDER
* WALLPAPER TABLE OR COVERED SURFACE FOR PASTING
* SPIRIT LEVEL OR TAPE MEASURE

Patchwork wallpaper

Old wallpaper can rarely be found in quantities large enough to cover a whole room, but by patching your way around the walls you can combine single rolls and oddments of favourite papers to very pretty effect. If you like things to be perfect you can measure a grid onto the wall before you begin, or simply layer your patches, of same or different sizes, until you have covered the wall without a gap. Add together the lengths of each roll to make sure you have enough to cover all the area you wish to.

The surface of the wall needs to be smooth, dust-free and clean before you begin so that the papers stick well and your finished wall is neat and tidy.

1. Begin by cutting the papers. You could paper stripes of different papers around the wall, or any size of square from roll width, down to tiny labour-of-love, matchbox-sized pieces. The squares pictured are approximately 15cm square as a guide. Use a guillotine or a steel rule, craft knife and cutting board to cut even-sized pieces. When you have enough to cover the area you are working on you can plot out your lines.

2. Use a weight and a long piece of string, or plumb line, to chalk vertical lines at intervals along the wall. The more perfect an effect you are after, the more lines for guidance you will need. (I didn't use any....)

3. Use a spirit level to add horizontal lines, or measure and join together points of the same height at varying places along the wall. When you are confident that you have enough lines in place you can begin to paper.

4. Choose and plan your design. The one pictured is randomly placed, just with no two adjoining papers of the same pattern. If you want a more structured look to the wall, lay out the pieces and make a plan for each area before you start sticking. Looking at original vintage and antique textile patchworks is good for ideas.

5. When you are ready, apply paste to the back of the pieces and smooth them into place, starting at a top corner. Work your way along the rows, either vertically or horizontally, just overlapping each piece as you go. Use the grid lines to keep the rows on track as you progress. Use a soft, dry brush to smooth out any wrinkles or air bubbles as you progress. Adjoining rows should also overlap a little bit. Keep going until the whole area is covered.

Teacup lights

For a very long time whatever our ancestors did, it would seem they had a cup of tea just before or just afterwards, such are the number of old teacups that turn up at sales, thrift shops and markets. We have a great collection in our house for drinking out of, another load that sit on the dresser just looking beautiful, and now we also have a fantastic assortment that hang from hooks and branches all around the house and garden, each with a tea light inside, throwing a warm light from a pretty vessel.

A sensible approach is needed when deciding where it is safe to hang them, and as ever, when candles are lit, they should not be left burning in a room without supervision or, in this case, be positioned near hanging fabrics, or where children are tempted to play with them. Make sure that the candle flame is at least 40cm below the ceiling, branches or under a garden umbrella.

1. Each teacup needs its own wire cage, a little bit like the wire around a champagne cork. Trim the garden wire into 50cm lengths - you will need two per cup. Turn the cup upside down on a table with the handle towards you.

Align two wires either side of the cup, then twist them together on each side of the lip on the base to form a tight clasp on the cups. The handle should be towards you and the wires sticking out either side.

2. Turn the cup by 90 degrees, split the wires where they are twisted and pull one from each side so the next twist can be made by the rim of the cup. One twist will be by the handle and the other opposite. Twist again and the cup should now have a secure wire cage around it.

3. Add a wire frame to as many cups as you wish to hang from your frame. Attach the cups one by one to the wire wreath ring. Tightly twist the wires to the inner and outer rings so that each cup is attached in four places bending the wires over the rings, then tightly around until you have a secure hanging point. Balance the ring on a vase or similar so that you can add all the cups and keep the wires straight.

4. Make sure that the cups are evenly balanced, then add a hanger using two long pieces of wire (check where you are hanging and measure the wire accordingly) twisted together and with their ends attached at four points to the outer ring. Hang it in place on a solid hook or branch, then add a tea light to each cup. Light them and the fine china will glow in the candlelight.

Brightening up your bathroom

It is so relaxing to have beautiful things around you when you bathe. You do not need a palace or the perfect bathroom to create a cool chamber in which to soak in the tub. I have lived with plastic tubs and vile tiles for years before saving up the time and money to replace perfectly serviceable bathrooms with something lovely, so have got into the habit of making the most of the smallest room in the house.

FURNITURE

Adding any sort of furniture to a bathroom can help to prettify it. Floor-standing shelves are very useful and look great stacked with towels and toiletries. Make room for a chair or a stool, if you can. Having somewhere to sit and relax in the bathroom feels very decadent. If your bathroom is on the small side, consider an enormous mirror leaning against or hanging on a wall, which can add a wonderful feeling of space.

WALL COVERINGS

Colourful wallpapers and bright, beautiful paints on untiled walls and ceilings offer a cost-effective way of transforming the look of a bathroom. As bathrooms are normally on the small and cosy side, it is often more affordable to splash out on your favourite or more expensive wallpapers and paints. Check that they are suitable for bathrooms.

Outdated tiles can be painted over, but few finishes are terribly effective or long-lasting. If you have a truly shocking set of tiles that make the mere thought of a candlelit bath a nightmare, try using the chalk paint described on page 20 and distress and wax it to pre-empt the inevitable scratches and marks that will eventually appear.

DISPLAYS

If you can add picture hooks or fixings to your walls, bathrooms can be great places for displaying favourite items such as pictures, plates, baskets and all sorts of collections. Choose china with similar colours or shapes, and pictures with a common theme. Gather large shells or dishes and choose objects that can withstand the humidity of the bathroom and are easy to take down and dust. Having baskets and boxes with lids allows you to hide away toiletries and potions for when visitors use the bathroom.

YOU WILL NEED:

CHINA VESSELS WITH LIDS * HEAVY PEBBLES OR
OLD WEIGHTS * PLASTER OF PARIS * RUBBER GLOVES
* OLD MIXING BOWL OR LARGE JUG * OLD SPOON
FOR STIRRING * INSTANT ADHESIVE

Plaster of Paris bookends

I have wanted to make these for ages. As the owner of more than my fair share of china, I have the odd teapot with a chipped spout and terrine with a crack that are therefore no longer suitable for using for their original purpose, yet are still lovely to look at. So rather than throw them away or smash them into crocks for garden pots, why not turn them, with the addition of plaster of Paris, into bookends, so you can admire them for longer? Larger pieces can be put to good use as doorstops. Be warned with this project, the china will sometimes split as the mixture dries but the plaster will hold all the pieces together.

1. Clean and dry the outside of the vessel thoroughly. Put a few heavy stones or old weights into the bottom of the vessel, but well below the top line of where the plaster of Paris will sit.

2. Mix up the plaster in an old bowl or plastic jug according to the packet instructions. Make sure that you use rubber gloves and avoid placing your hands into the plaster as it can become very hot during the curing process. When you have a smooth mixture, carefully pour it into the vessel and tap it gently to remove any air bubbles. Leave it for 24 hours to ensure it is totally set.

3. Attach any lids (e.g. for a teapot) with superglue so that they cannot be removed. Use as a bookend or doorstop.

Dressing table four ways

If your dressing table is one of the first things you see in the morning, you might as well make sure that it is one of the most inspiring. These little vignettes are some of my favourite things, but you can gather together your best bits to group into eye-pleasing little collections.

Change your look with the seasons, with the arrival of new vintage finds, or clear the decks for a few weeks in between whilst seeking vintage inspiration.

If you have the chance, add some seasonal flowers to your table too. It puts perspective into the year if you see a snowdrop there one day, a first narcissus, lily of the valley or a fat little bunch of sweet peas. The humble daisy, plucked from a cottage lawn and popped by the clump into a tiny pot or old glass bottle can be as charming as a bowl of roses. Stronger garden herbs like bay and rosemary are around all year to add a little greenery or seek out old millinery decorations of blooms made from ribbons and silks when winter months leave gardens bare of blossom.

You can choose your look according to the season, or just arrange collections of your favourite things to gladden the eye.

SPRING IS IN THE AIR

This blue selection of china and trinkets and French floral wallpaper looks lovely together. Have candles ready for restful evenings and you can continue the colour theme to bedding and curtains if you wish.

CUT GLASS AND SILVER

The gilt, glass and slightly Victorian style setting gathers up finials and fragments from old mirrors with some pieces inspired by nature. Old and reproduction glass domes can be carefully brought home from vintage markets and can stand over anything from children's first shoes to your favourite jewellery.

VICTORIAN GILT

Spring time colours and pretty things brighten up any morning. Add rose patterned wallpaper, floral fabrics and colourful china to make your dressing table sing.

VIOLETS ARE BLUE

Cool and crisp silvery trinkets and white china have a wintery feel. Mix and match modern and vintage, keep an eye out for pieces to fit into each vignette and change the scene when the weather warms up.

**EATING
AND
DINING**

Drying herbs and making teabags

DRYING HERBS

Gather little bunches of herbs such as sage, mint, marjoram, thyme, bay, rosemary, lemon balm, fennel and dill. Make sure they are good fresh herbs, free from dirt and dust. Lightly tie each one into a bunch with kitchen string and hang them up, well spaced out, somewhere warm, dry and airy until they are brittle and dry. Inspect them carefully to make sure that they are all dry and then gently crumble them onto a sheet of paper and tip them into scrupulously clean and dry jam jars.

TEABAGS

1. Measure out a rectangle 15cm x 10cm and make a template. Iron the muslin fabric and then cut around this lots of times to make the little pouches. Fold over a 1cm hem, with the thread or fine string tucked inside it, along one of the long sides, with the thread sticking out at each end. Iron it in place.

2. Make a little pile like this and then start to sew. Use running stitch to whizz along the hem, with the thread inside the channel, but not catching it along the top of each sachet. Then fold them in half, all wrong sides together with the hem at the top and sew around the two remaining sides, starting just under where the drawstrings emerge.

3. Turn the sachets right side around and tie the ends of the threads together to form the drawstring.

4. Place the sachets into another jar, ready to accompany the dried herbs. Add labels inside the jar on a little pretty piece of paper.

5. Fill the sachets with herbs to make teas or a savoury selection to flavour stews and casseroles. Remove the bag before you eat!

BOUQUET GARNI

A little bundle of herbs and flavours you can make them up and dry them as a bundle without a sachet if you wish.

Take a bay leaf and add a little sprig of each herb and a curl of orange or lemon zest trimmed from the fruit with a sharp potato peeler if you wish, and then tie the bundle in place. String several up at a time to dry.

Kitchenalia

'Kitchenalia' is a general term used to describe utensils and other useful items found in the kitchen, and the vintage variety of kitchenalia is available in abundance, often cheap and invariably useful.

If you are buying old items that you plan to use, ensure that any surfaces that will come into contact with food are sound, rust- or chip-free and up to the task they are intended for.

As with pretty much anything that comes into the house that is secondhand, hot soapy water and a good scrub before use are essential. Putting your goods through a couple of cycles in the dishwasher, if you feel they are dishwasher safe, is also advisable.

YOU WILL NEED:

....

FABRIC DYE AND DYEING EQUIPMENT * WEIGHING SCALES
* TABLECLOTH WITH LACY EDGING * FABRIC SCISSORS OR
STITCH PICKER * IRON * PINS * SEWING MACHINE OR
HAND-SEWING NEEDLE * SEWING THREAD

....

TO ADD TRIMMINGS YOU WILL ALSO NEED: FABRIC SCISSORS
* STITCH PICKER (OPTIONAL) * LACE TRIMMING * FABRIC DYE
(OPTIONAL) * TAPE MEASURE * FABRIC FOR TABLECLOTH
* IRON * PINS * SEWING MACHINE * SEWING THREAD

Tablecloths and napkins

Back in the day, a bare table was a rare thing. Starchy damask was ironed immaculately and set in place on the dining table before dinner settings were laid upon it. Squares of linen were edged with hand crochet and lace. Hours were spent embroidering flowers and garlands and ladies in crinolines onto tea cloths. Seersucker wrinkled on the tables in the fifties and sixties and then, suddenly, we pretty much stopped using these previously essential items of sophisticated dining.

A consequence of their previous ubiquity is that there are hoards of tablecloths to be gathered up and used, but not all are in perfect condition. The ideas below will help you to breathe new life into old cloths that have been damaged or marked over the years. You can experiment with different fabric dyes, from little chemical sachets that you mix with salt and water for instant rainbows of colour, to using cauldron-like pots

with onion skins, beetroot and roots all set with natural mordants such as alum.

1. Decide what type and colour of dye you are using and weigh the fabric to ensure that the quantity of dye you have is enough to colour the entire cloth evenly. If there are lots of marks on the fabric, choose a shade that is richer and darker than the existing colour to mask them. Unpick the edging of the cloth if you would like a contrasting coloured trim.

2. Follow the packet instructions for your dye and colour the cloth and the edging in different shades. When you have completed the process, wash and dry both the fabric and trim to make sure they are colourfast.

3. Iron both the cloth and the trim really well, then pin the trim back in place. Sew it onto the cloth using a sewing machine or by hand, if you prefer, removing the pins as you go. Iron the fabric and trim again, then fold it up neatly ready for teatime.

ADDING TRIMS TO FABRIC

Pretty crochet and lace edgings can be reused even if the tablecloth itself is tired and worn. Carefully reclaim the trimming from the damaged cloth by unpicking or cutting along the seam. Discard the worn cloth or save good areas for making napkins or other projects. Alternatively, online auction sites often sell lace trimmings, some made years ago but never used, and a rummage at markets and thrift shops may yield rich pickings if you are lucky.

1. If you would like to colour the trimming, follow the packet instructions for your chosen dye, then wash, dry and iron the edging.

2. If you have an entire square or circle of reclaimed trimming, measure the interior edge when the edging is spread out to get the dimensions for your new fabric. This measurement is the size your hemmed cloth must be to fit within the reclaimed trimming, so add a couple of centimetres in every direction to allow for hemming. If you have a length of pretty edging you can add it to both ends of your cloth. Measure the length of the trim and divide this measurement in two. Hem the edges by turning over a couple of centimetres on each end and sewing in place.

3. Cut your pretty fabric to the right size. Turn over a 1cm double hem (fold it over once at a centimetre and then again, so that all the raw edges are hidden) along each edge. For a neat finish at the corners, cut just over 2cm off the corner at a 45 degree angle to the corner to give a smart mitred finish without too much bulky fabric.

4. Iron and pin the hems, then sew all around, removing the pins as you go. Spread out your hemmed fabric with the right side facing up. Place the trimming over the edges so that it fractionally overlaps the edges of the cloth. Pin the trimming in place, then sew it neatly onto the cloth, just where they overlap. Remove the pins and press well.

TIP You can make napkins in just the same way, but on a smaller scale. If you need to cut any lace or crochet edgings, turn over a little hem on the trimming and sew it in place to prevent fraying.

INGREDIENTS FOR BREAD OR BREAD PACKET MIXTURE * CLEAN
TERRACOTTA FLOWERPOTS (EIGHT 7.5CM OR THREE 12.5CM) * SALT
* OLIVE OIL * KITCHEN PAPER OR CLEAN CLOTH * MIXING BOWL
* MEASURING JUG * WOODEN SPOON * SCALES * MEASURING
SPOONS * COOLING RACK * SIEVE * KNIFE * TEA TOWEL

Flowerpot loaves

*I am sure you can find lots of reasons why it is
not a good idea to make a loaf of bread in a
flowerpot, but when I was growing up these were
a real treat. Whenever bread was about to be
made, we raced around the garden trying to
find a terracotta pot that was small, whole and
empty for our baby loaves and be back in time
to give it a scrub and pop in the dough to rise.*

PROOFING THE POTS

The pots need to have a really good scrub before you can
use them for cooking. Send them through the dishwasher
or wash thoroughly by hand. Let them dry completely, then
dab a little olive oil on a folded sheet of kitchen paper or a
clean cloth, dip it in salt and rub it around the inside of the
pot. Place the pots upside down on a baking tray and pop
them into a hot oven (150°C) for 15 minutes so they are
clean and sealed.

RICH BROWN BREAD

1. Use a bread recipe or a packet of bread mix to make one
   loaf. This normally makes around eight mini loaves in
   7.5cm pots or three in 12.5cm pots. Read through the whole
   recipe first, then make it up to the point where you need to
   shape the dough before cooking.

2. Cut the dough into eight or three equal pieces, depending
   on the size of flowerpots you are using. Now carefully fold
   all the outside edges of each piece of dough inwards until
   you have a piece with a round, smooth top. Mould it into
   a cone shape and drop it into the flowerpot, dome-side up.
   Cut a little cross on the top of the dough in each pot using
   a sharp knife. Transfer the pots to a warm place, cover with
   a clean tea towel and leave to rise until the dough reaches
   above the rims of the pots.

3. Cook in a preheated oven according to the recipe for
   around 20 minutes, or a little longer for the larger pots,
   until the dough has risen and is beginning to brown on
   the surface. The sides should release from the pot and

sound hollow when tapped. If the loaves feel a little soft still, ease them out of the pots and return them to the oven for a couple of minutes more.

4. When you are happy the loaves are cooked, turn them out of the pots and leave them to cool on a wire rack. Dust the tops with a little flour, if you wish. If you can resist eating them straightaway, allow to cool, place them back into their flowerpots and serve.

Edged towels

Plain tea towels offer the tempting opportunity to add pattern and detail to your kitchen - a colourfully edged towel brightens up a kitchen in much the same way as a pretty bath towel does a bathroom. Trimmings can be ribbons, lace edgings, ric rac, bobbles, bias binding or hemmed strips of fabric - vintage and reclaimed fabrics will add to the vintage vibe.

1. Ensure that the towel and trimming you are using are both colourfast and prewashed so that they do not bleed colour or shrink when the finished towel is washed. Hot wash the towel and trimming separately before you begin, then dry and iron them.

2. If your trimming has raw edges, these must be hemmed before you stitch them in place on the towel. Measure the width of the towel and then turn over ends of ribbons or cut edges of crochet or lace and sew them in place with a similar coloured thread so that they are the width of the towel.

If you are using fabric to make your own trimming, perhaps to match your curtains or wallpaper, turn over hems on a piece of fabric to create a little panel the same width as the tea towel, then iron and stitch the hems in place.

3. Pin the lengths of trimming to the edges of the towel on the right side. Sew each length of trimming in place. If you are using lace or crochet edging, place the trim with the right side facing down and with the straight edge about 1cm from the edge of the towel and sew it in place. Iron it back so that the right side is now facing upwards and stitch the edging to the towel again – about 0.5cm from the towel's edge.

TIP You can dye crochet or lace edging too before you sew it in place. Use cold water dye, made up to instructions on the packet and dye, wash and iron the trimmings. Wash them well before you attach to the towel to prevent colours running. Try this project with bath towels too.

YOU WILL NEED:

SMALL DISHES AND OTHER ITEMS SUCH AS SAUCERS, PLATES,
SAUCE TERRINES, LARGE STEMMED GLASSES, PRETTY BOWLS,
LITTLE BASINS, CUPS, VASES, COMPOTES, CHOPPING BOARDS
AND SPOONS

Meze and small plates

*Supper with friends can become a complicated
display of culinary prowess, or a stressful journey
through the early part of the evening with a
cookbook in one hand and a far-too-quickly
emptying glass of wine in the other. And that's
before people have sat down to reveal their
allergies, dietary requirements and special
catering needs. Small-dish eating saves you
from having to deal with all sorts of potential
problems at the last minute.*

*We eat like this pretty much all year round,
with the additions of small casseroles of meats,
chicken or beans and layered pasta dishes to
fend off the cold of winter.*

There is no need to limit the small-plates approach to
savoury dishes either – desserts are pretty as a picture
served in a teacup, or look very dainty presented in a
champagne saucer. Embrace the saying 'a little bit of
what you fancy does you good', which is pretty much
my mantra for living the good life.

An eclectic selection of vintage dishes full of tempting
morsels looks lovely spread out on a dining table and
offer a little nod to good old-fashioned favourite foods.
Basically, anything goes – dishes of different shapes,
sizes and heights all add interest to the table. Ensure
any old dishes are washed really well first, and only put
hot food into pots that are robust enough for the job.

Some dishes suit small-plate dining better than others.
Below is a list of suggestions for suitable fare to get
you started:

· hummus and vases of grissini

· roasted red peppers with garlic and olive oil

· little pots of olives, capers, toasted pine nuts,
  croutons and Parmesan shavings

· new potatoes with mint dressing

· ruffles of Parma ham and salami with figs

· flakes of cold-poached salmon with lemons
  wrapped in muslin

· soft goat's cheese with heaps of freshly ground
  black pepper and olive oil

· halved grapes, crumbled Stilton, toasted pecan
  nuts and radicchio

- little jugs of balsamic vinegar and olive oil dressing
- grilled artichokes
- slow-roasted tomatoes with mozzarella
- avocado vinaigrette
- smoked chicken and crispy lettuce Caesar salad
- rocket salad with edible flower petals
- summer prawn cocktail with shredded lettuce and Marie Rose sauce
- smoked salmon, soured cream, chives and finely chopped shallots
- warm buttered blinis
- hot prawns with garlic butter
- butter beans dressed with lemon juice, truffle oil and lots of chopped parsley
- fine slivers of rare roast beef with crème fraîche and horseradish cream
- couscous jewelled with apricots, roasted courgettes, mint, coriander and lemon zest
- tiny pots of harissa or chilli sauce
- Coronation chicken salad with toasted almonds and fresh mango
- warm asparagus with melted butter.

Pick a selection of the above, then pot up each dish onto tiny plates. Put all the dishes that are best served at room temperature down in the middle of the table just before your guests arrive. Anything that is best served chilled, such as salmon or prawns, should be potted, covered and refrigerated until you and your guests are ready to eat. Have a couple of hot dishes ready to pop into the oven or a pan, which you can then transfer into a pot to put on the table at the last minute. Encourage your guests to pass around the little dishes and graze on the food.

For desserts, pile up tiny éclairs onto stands, fill elegant glasses with jellies, make mock crumbles by spooning fruit compotes into glasses and topping with cooked crumble mixture and use teacups as serving bowls for other desserts too.

Finally, serve platters of cheese and you should find that everyone has managed to enjoy a little bit of what they fancy.

Hand-cranked machines

There is a broad range of beautiful vintage hand-cranked kitchen gadgets out there, waiting to be found – marvellous machines that use manpower to chop, grate and grind. They come in many colours finished in soft enamels, shiny metals or glossy black, often with gold lettering.

Search out these marvellous machines at markets and in thrift shops. Look out for mincers, marmalade shredders, bean slicers, apple corers, graters, coffee grinders, butter churners, egg beaters and flour sifters.

Inspect your finds thoroughly to check there are no obvious missing pieces (mincers, in particular, need to be bristling with bits before they work properly). Most were made before modern health and safety rules applied, so beware of exposed cutting blades and grinders and keep small fingers well out of the way. That said, our children always cut the beans and grind the coffee. I particularly like the effort that has to be put in to turn these machines and feel it is yet anther reason not to have to go to the gym. Live the dream, with elbow grease!

Enamelware

Pretty as a picture, but not great if you drop it – this just about sums up enamelware. Vintage enamelware has a charm all of its own. Colanders and bread crocks, pots, pans, ladles and jugs were made in enamel as standard and in such huge quantities that today you can still find original bits and pieces in charity shops and antique markets.

When it comes to enamelware, condition is everything, so if you find a perfect pitcher or a colander that has made it through a century of draining without so much as a chip, you have got yourself a good find. Older enamel tends to be heavier, with a distinctly retro collection of not-quite-pastel colours often featuring alongside bright reds and acid yellows.

Check any pieces that you buy to ensure the cooking surfaces are intact as rust is not good to eat! Chips and cracks on the outside are fine, but interiors should be chip-free or priced accordingly and used as decorative pieces only.

Watermarks, rust stains and cooking marks may have taken their toll on older pieces. Soak them overnight in a mixture of one part vinegar to three parts water, then wash thoroughly in warm soapy water. Alternatively, use oven-cleaning materials, but avoid metal scourers that could damage the enamel.

If all else fails, seal corroded areas with a little cooking oil, polish them well and hang them high in the kitchen where no one will notice the odd imperfection on an otherwise beautiful piece.

Dining table four ways

If you have a passion for vintage china like me, entertaining is a great opportunity to show off. A few simple lettuce leaves never looked more beautiful than arranged onto a fabulous cabbage design and you won't want to serve a sponge on a simple plate again, once you have a vintage cake stand nestling in your plate armoury.

If you can, abandon any fears about matching sets, which knife goes where, or the size of glasses. Stack, layer, line up and arrange your table until it is bristling with vintage pieces. If formal is the only way, and matching is a must, pick a colour or style of crockery if a dinner service is not at your disposal. The white and green plates overleaf look as though they were made, probably close to two centuries ago, with dessert in mind, but look lovely for a salad.

Old crockery, glassware and cutlery were almost certainly not made to withstand the temperature of a dishwasher so precious pieces should be washed by hand. Bone-handled knives are particularly prone to coming apart if they go through a cycle by mistake, so take care when clearing away your favourite things. Wash everything in lots of warm soapy water and use a good linen tea towel to dry everything properly afterwards. I always think that it is better to use lovely plates, dishes and proper old glasses than leave them tucked up inside the cupboard. Even when very young our children had their own favourite plates. And instead of discussions about the princess plate or the orange one, we always have 'I want the Meissen' or 'Pass me the Derby'. You have to start them young you know!

Here there are four different looks for making the table a talking point.

CABBAGE PATCH

Lovely Victoria who designed this book has a collection of cabbageware that looks stunning on a green table set with luscious food. Choose a particular style of china like this to collect and you will be surprised how often examples turn up. Wonderful Wedgwood to modern majolica copies are all out there to find.

BRIGHT AND BEAUTIFUL

The diminishing cut coloured glassware is grouped with plates and flowers of matching colours to set this floral table. A length of vintage linen makes a fabulous tablecloth and every place setting has a colour of its own.

HOME IN TIME FOR TEA

This eclectic take on an afternoon tea table shows how to go about mixing and matching old tea sets, ditsy rose tablecloths and cake stands. Think pretty, fine and dainty, make some proper tea and pile into some crumpets.

NEARLY SMART

For high days and holidays this more formal setting uses sets of plates and cutlery that actually match. Try using old jelly moulds to arrange your flowers, trawl through charity shops and car boot sales for similar style bone-handled cutlery and use old decanters for wine and water. Add candelabra for evening dining and polish up anything silvery.

SLEEPING
AND
BATHING

YOU WILL NEED:
....
BOLSTER CUSHION OR BOLSTER CUSHION PAD * TAPE
MEASURE * NEWSPAPER, PENCIL, STICKY TAPE AND
PAPER SCISSORS FOR MAKING THE PATTERN * SCRAPS
AND LENGTHS OF FABRIC * TAILOR'S CHALK * FABRIC
SCISSORS * PINS * SEWING MACHINE * SEWING THREADS
* IRON * RIBBONS

Bolster cushions

*I have this idyllic image of sitting up in bed
drinking some exotic tea from a dainty teacup,
my husband reading his perfectly ironed
broadsheet newspaper, small children happily
playing on the rug next to the bed. Propping us
up are several large bolsters covered in fine
fabric and stuffed with pure goose down.
This is not something that ever seems to
happen all at once in our busy, messy home,
but the bolster bit is achievable. I'm not
crazy about round sausage-shaped bolsters,
but the extended pillow variety is really
comfortable and useful - and not just for beds.
These long cushions look great across the
back of the sofa or on a bench in the garden.*

1. Bolster pillows and pillow pads are available in a variety
of lengths. Choose one that fits right across your bed,
stretch it out fully and measure its length and width to
obtain the dimensions you need for your finished cover.

2. Make a pattern to the exact size of the cushion out of
newspaper, taped together if necessary. Your cushion
cover needs to be a centimetre or so smaller than the pad
along each edge for a plump-looking cushion, so if your
front and back cushion panels are the same size as the
finished cushion, and you sew them together with a 1cm
seam allowance, then by the time you have sewn them
together they will be the right size. Now make a smaller
pattern piece for the vertical stripes on your bolster.
For this, use the measurement of the cushion plus
about 20cm.

3. Use the smaller pattern piece to cut strips of fabric to
patchwork together. Use combinations of your favourite
fabrics of roughly the same weight. Different textures,
such as velvet, linen and blanket fabric, work well
together. It is helpful if you have washed the fabrics and

know that they are colourfast, so you can be reassured that the colours will not run when it comes to cleaning your bolster cover.

4. Lay out these strips across the long bolster pattern with each piece overlapping by 1cm to allow for seam allowances, until you have enough to cover the pattern. Then sew the patchwork together. Place the first two pieces with right sides together and lined up along the edges to be joined. Pin them in place, then sew them together using running stitch, removing the pins as you go. Repeat until you have a long strip of fabric that perfectly fits your pattern.

5. For the back panel, you can use one strip of fabric, cut to size using the template or repeat the patchwork process to make a patchwork back. When you have finished, iron the panels well, ironing the seams flat. Turn a double hem over at one end, pin, iron and sew in place one end.

6. This pillow uses the 'housewife closure' method, which consists of a simple extra panel of fabric attached to the front panel at the open end of the cushion cover to tuck the pillow into, much like many pillowcases. To make this extra panel, cut one more piece of fabric using the smaller

pattern, turn over a double hem at one end, pin the hem in place, then sew it using running stitch.

7. Lay out the front panel with the right side facing up. Next, align the housewife panel on the left hand side, with the right side facing down and the unhemmed edge lined up with the left hand edge of the front piece. Then place the back panel on top with the right side facing down, and the hemmed end at the housewife end too, just short of the line where you will stitch. Pin the panels together. Using running stitch, sew all around the four sides, working with a 1cm seam allowance.

8. To make for a smarter finish, cut away the spare fabric at the point of each corner, press all the seams open then turn the fabric so that the right sides face out. Feed in the cushion pad and tuck the end behind the housewife panel. For a neater closure you can sew a couple of lengths of ribbon to each end and tie them in a bow. Finally, lay the cushion across the top of your bed, wait for Sunday and hope for that Lapsang Souchong moment.

Duvet cover

Most modern fabrics do not come in a width that allows you to make an un-joined duvet cover for a double bed and, even if you manage to find fabrics that are wide enough, the sheer quantity of fabric required would make the exercise quite expensive. Making covers from old sheets is simple and cost effective. Look out for sheets with pretty edgings to add good detail, and wash and iron them before you begin. Depending on the size of the sheet, you may also have leftover fabric to make matching pillowcases.

1. Align the two sheets with their wrong sides facing down on a clean floor. If there is a pretty edge to the sheet, place this at the foot end and make sure that it line up neatly with a hemmed or pretty edge from the other sheet. Place your duvet onto the sheet and draw all around it in tailor's chalk the chalk lines, but also within these lines, right into the central area of the duvet cover, to ensure that the sheets cannot move out of alignment when they are being sewn.

Once the seam allowances have been taken off, the cover will be smaller than the duvet, which makes for a good, plump-looking fit. Pin the top and bottom sheets together near the chalk lines, and in the central area to ensure the sheets cannot move when they are being sewn.

2. Cut along the chalk lines and then sew the three closed edges of the duvet cover together, working with a 1cm seam allowance and removing the pins as you go. Turn the cover so that the right sides are facing out, carefully pushing out the corners. For a super neat finish and to prevent any loose threads tangling during washing, sew another line of stitches about 2cm all around the three open sides, enclosing the cut edges inside of the fabric and making a smart trim around the edge.

3. With the cover still right sides around, sew roughly one third of the way in from each side at the open end, just by the existing hem of the sheet, leaving a gap to feed the duvet into.

Eiderdowns and Blankets

If they are lovely and perfect, I will happily sleep on secondhand sheets. I buy all sorts of old linens, bring them home and boil them! Twice. Some people recoil in horror at the thought of sleeping on someone else's sheets. When they do, I always ask them where they remember having their most luxurious getting-into-bed experience. The answer is normally at some lovely hotel, where they have curled up on sheets slept on by hundreds of different people...

Obviously, these items do not have to be vintage, but making up beds with sheets, blankets and eiderdowns, particularly for guests, gives a luxurious feeling, so it is well worth gathering up a little linen cupboard of pretty things for just this occasion. Use your fabulous bolster cushions (see page 140), old patchwork bedcovers, your best and most plump pillows and your chintziest eiderdowns to give your guests a warm welcome to night-time in your home.

When making up a bed, start with a big, well-ironed bottom sheet, tucked in really well. The perfect way to tuck in a sheet is with 'hospital corners', in which the sheet is carefully folded back on itself to make the most secure and neatest tuck.

Next, put on two or four plump pillows and a big top sheet with plenty of extra fabric at the top end. Then add a blanket, fold over the top of the sheet and tuck this in with the blanket. Tuck the blanket in all the way around. Top with a bedcover or eiderdown and your bolster and some pretty cushions or lavender bags for the perfect finishing touches.

OLD WOOLLEN BLANKET * STITCH PICKER (IF NECESSARY) * FABRIC
SCISSORS * SEWING MACHINE OR HAND-SEWING NEEDLE * SEWING
THREAD * FABRIC SCRAPS FOR PATCHES (IF NECESSARY) * COMPASS
OR CIRCULAR OBJECT, CARD, PENCIL AND PAPER SCISSORS FOR
MAKING TEMPLATE (OPTIONAL) * TAILOR'S CHALK OR FABRIC
MARKER (OPTIONAL)

Scalloped edge blankets

You have to love a scalloped edge. I want them on my wallpaper, around the edges of painted floors, in the garden and on my bedclothes. This pretty detail softens the edges of walls, bedding and even clothes. Layered over other colourful bedding, the effect can be stunning.

There are heaps of old woollen blankets out there with frayed and tatty edges and giving them a scalloped edge is a very simple and effective way of neatening them up. All wool blankets that are woven rather than knitted are suitable for this project. And there's no need to be put off if the blanket has a mark or hole in it - you can resurrect it by sewing patches of pretty fabric over them, whether they are on the front or the back of the blanket.

1. If you have a good eye and are working without a template, lay out your blanket and cut little half circle shapes along the edges. Without having marked them out first, they may not all be exactly the same, but the effect will still be charming. If you have made a template, line up the straight edge of your scallop template with the straight edge of your blanket and chalk around the template, continuing the pattern around the entire edge of the blanket to make your cutting guide. You can cut a full scallop at the corners or an indent depending where the pattern falls.

2. Cut along the outline to create your pretty edging. If your blanket has been felted there should not be any fraying edges.

TIP If the blanket you have is slightly itchy, leave one edge unscalloped. Take a length of hemmed fabric that is wide enough to encase the edge, fold it in half lengthways, iron the fold, then position it along the unscalloped edge of the blanket to recreate the satin trimming. Sew the new trimming in place.

YOU WILL NEED:

SELECTION OF SCARVES OF ROUGHLY THE SAME SIZE
* PINS * SEWING MACHINE * SEWING THREAD * IRON
* CURTAIN WIRE AND HOOKS OR STRONG RIBBON
AND DRAWING PINS

Silk scarf curtains

Being so far out of fashion, many beautiful silk scarves are kept folded up in drawers and never see the light of day. This era-defining fashion accessory that no woman would be without in the 1950s and 60s desperately needs a new purpose - why not combine a few to make a curtain? A light, silky panel made of delicate silk scarves can make a very effective window dressing. Choose your squares with the colour of your room in mind. Light, sheer scarves work well in place of net curtains and rich, dark tones are great for curtains that will be drawn open during the day. Thankfully, many scarves are of a similar size, usually around 60sq cm, so joining them together is easy, if a little slippery.

1. Lay out the scarves on a large surface or on a sheet spread out on the floor. Now decide on the positioning of each scarf in the curtain - move them all around on the sheet until you are satisfied with the composition.

2. Now begin to sew the scarves together, one vertical row at a time. Align the first two scarves to be joined with their right sides facing and pin them together along the edges that are to be joined. Sew them together, removing the pins as you go, sewing close to the finished edge of the scarves.

Next, attach another scarf to the row using the same process. Repeat the process until you have all the strips of scarves you need to make your curtain design.

3. You can trim off any edges that are not quite the same width so that the strips are all the same size. Then begin to join the strips in the same way as you did the individual scarves until you have one large panel.

4. Iron the curtain, opening out the seams on the back so that they sit flat, then press a 2cm hem along the top edge of the curtain. Pin it in place and sew down the hem, removing the pins as you go, producing a channel in which to thread the curtain wire or ribbon.

5. Feed the curtain wire through the channel at the top of the curtain. If you are using ribbon, hook a large safety pin through one end of the ribbon and push it into and along the hemmed edge, and out the other side. Ruffle the curtain evenly along the wire or ribbon.

6. If you have used curtain wire, attach the hooks into the frame of the window where the curtain is to hang and stretch the wire taut between them. If you have used ribbon, use heavy drawing pins to secure the ribbon across the window frame.

PAPER, PENCIL, RULER AND PAPER SCISSORS FOR MAKING TEMPLATE
* IRON * MUSLIN * TAILOR'S CHALK * FABRIC SCISSORS * SEWING
MACHINE OR HAND-SEWING NEEDLE * SEWING THREAD * FINE
STRING OR STRONG THREAD CUT INTO 20CM LENGTHS * PINS
* DRIED HERBS, FLOWERS AND LEAVES * JAM JARS, ACCOMPANYING
FABRIC TOPS AND LABELS

Muslin bath sachets

We have a big, old cast-iron bath at home, with claw feet, gently worn enamel and an old-fashioned wooden rack that sits over the tub to hold your book, coffee or soap. And every so often I run a totally decadent, completely full, really steamy bath perfumed with aromatic scents and have a long soak and a big think.

In the past I have floated rose petals, lavender flowers and even geranium leaves in the bath for an instant blast of fragrance. However, as I also have to clean the bath, I have taken to making little packets of dried flowers and herbs instead – tea bags for the bath. My favourite fragrances and combinations are calming lavender and soothing camomile, but bear in mind that there are some herbs and flowers that should be avoided if you are pregnant or if laying on a bath for a child.

1. First, make the template. Measure out a 15cm x 10cm rectangle on paper and cut it out. Iron the muslin, then chalk several times around your template on the fabric and cut out the shapes. On each rectangle, fold over a 1cm hem along one long edge, catching a length of thread or fine string within the hem, ensuring that the string sticks out at either end. Iron the hem in place. Continue in this way with all of the fabric rectangles until you have a little pile ready to sew.

2. Use running stitch to stitch down the hem on each rectangle, ensuring the thread remains inside the channel, but is not caught by the stitches. Then fold the sachets in half vertically with the wrong sides together and the hem at the top. Pin each one to secure, then sew around the open edges along the side and bottom of the pouch, starting just beneath the point at which the drawstrings emerge.

3. Turn each sachet so the right sides are facing out and tie the ends of the threads together to form the drawstring.

4. Pop the dried herbs, flowers and leaves into clean and carefully dried jam jars, topped with pretty fabric tops and place the little fabric sachets in another jar. Add labels inside the jars on small pieces of pretty paper. At bath time you can fill the sachets with your choice of dried herbs, flowers or leaves, depending on your mood.

Woollen pebble mat

Thick plain or old Welsh blankets make soft but hardwearing mats that are perfect for bedside or bathroom. This project takes a bit of time to make, but the finished effect is so pleasing, I think it is well worth the effort. Some old woollen blankets come in beautifully subtle natural shades that you can use for your mat, or you could design a pattern using a few colours and dye your cut pieces of wool in the bright and brilliant shades of your own design - wool takes colour very well.

The blanket you use to make your mat must be of a fairly tight weave. A hot machine wash will tighten up and slightly felt a blanket, if required. Either natural wool fleece or polyester stuffing can be used and you can vary the size of each pebble or keep things uniform.

TO MAKE A PATTERNED RUG

1. Plan a pattern for your rug by colouring squares on graph paper, using one square to represent one pebble. Simple yet effective designs to go for are spiral patterns for circular rugs, flowers or lines. To give you an idea of final size, each pebble will measure around 3–4cm across. Count the total number of pebbles you will need.

2. You could cut your circles freehand or, alternatively, use a template. To make the template, draw around a circular object with a 6–8cm diameter on a piece of card, then cut out the template. Lay the template on your fabric and chalk around the circumference as many times as you need to give you the required number of circles. Now cut out the circles following your guide lines.

3. As you generally use a weight of dye for a weight of fabric, it is most efficient to dye cut circles. Refer to your plan to establish the number of pebbles you need of each colour. There are many types of dye available, from natural dyes that produce a surprisingly varied palette to easy-to-use synthetic dyes in every shade. Follow the packet instructions of the dye that you choose, remembering to wear gloves and a suitable apron and to rinse out the fabric several times after you have dyed it. Lay out the dyed circles to dry.

4. Begin the stuffing process. Using good strong thread, sew a line of running stitch around the outside edge of each circle, working roughly 5mm in from the edge, then pull the thread to draw in the circle. Stuff the pouch created with lots of stuffing, then draw in the thread until you have closed the circle and created a little pebble. Stitch across the opening with plenty of stitches and tie off to secure. Now repeat the process until you have all the pebbles you need.

5. Attach the pebbles to one another by sewing right through the two pebbles you are attaching using a long needle and strong thread, then through all the adjacent pebbles in turn. Keep going until you have created your whole mat, referring to your design if and when necessary.

TO MAKE UNDYED RUGS

Cut the required number of circles from your blanket to create the dimension that you are after, as directed in step 2, then follow the sequence from step 4.

YOU WILL NEED:

APPLE CRATE OR BUSHEL BOX * MASKING TAPE * PAINT AND PAINTBRUSHES
(OPTIONAL) * TAPE MEASURE * FABRIC TO MAKE CURTAIN * FABRIC SCISSORS
* IRON * PINS * SEWING MACHINE * SEWING THREAD * CURTAIN WIRE AND HOOKS

TO MAKE THE WHISTLES & BELLS VERSION YOU WILL ALSO NEED:
PIECE OF SOFT WOOD FOR THE INTERIOR SHELF * BATTEN (APPROXIMATELY 15MM
X 30MM AND 70CM LONG) * PENCIL * HAND SAW * WOOD GLUE * SMALL PIN NAILS
* SMALL HAMMER

Bedside tables

It is good to have something at the side of the bed on which to rest an enormous breakfast bowl of coffee without fear of it tipping all over your favourite linen sheets. I have looked at many side tables over the years and I can honestly say that I don't love most of them, so beside all our beds are a somewhat random selection of trunks, suitcases, sewing boxes on legs, little stools, old wooden chairs and, my favourite, old apple crates, which lend themselves very well to being transformed into perfect bedside tables. There is a proper element of DIY to this project; you can make a very simple nightstand with a touch of paint and the addition of a little curtain, or go the whole hog, adding a useful interior shelf and even casters.

1. Give the apple crate a good wash and dry – leave it out in the sun or dry it on some newspaper next to a radiator. When it is totally dry, you can paint the inside, if required. Chalk paint makes a lovely finish – see page 20 for more details. Use masking tape to mask between the slats from the outside of the box so that the paint cannot leak out to the exterior when you paint inside the crate. Now paint the interior right up to the inside edges and allow the paint to dry completely, then remove the tape.

2. Stand the crate on its end and measure the front opening of the crate and cut a piece of fabric twice the width and about 10cm longer than the length of the opening. Turn over a hem 1cm on all sides, press and pin it in place before sewing all the way around. Turn over a large hem of around 3cm on the top of the curtain to make a channel for the wire. Pin and press that, too, then sew in place, removing the pins as you go.

3. Screw the little hooks that come with the curtain wire in place just behind the top edge of the box. Feed the wire through the double hem of the curtain. Stretch the wire across the box and hook the curtain in place.

WHISTLES AND BELLS VERSION

1. Give the apple crate a good wash and dry as described in step 1 above. To make a shelf for the box, cut a piece of wood to fit the interior of the box at the point at which you would like the shelf to sit. Builders' merchants will cut this to size, or you may have an old chopping board or tray that fits for a quick fix.

2. Measure the depth of the shelf to ascertain the length of the two battens you will need then mark out the required lengths on the battening in pencil. Now carefully cut the battens to the correct length using a hand saw.

3. Using wood glue, stick the battens in place on the sides of the crate at the point at which you want your shelf to sit. Then use small pin nails to hammer the battens firmly in place, from the inside of the crate.

4. When the glue has dried, slide the shelf in place.

Lampshade four ways

For simple seasonal updating, changing lampshades is the work of a moment. Our house is strewn with table lamps as overhead lighting is just far too bright for vintage living.

There are all sorts of courses and patterns that you can follow to create perfect shades. Drum types use specialist materials to create a shade, but I used the type of shade that has a metal frame with struts running between the top and bottom. The ideas here offer a few quirkier options, using simple-to-obtain materials that can be found around the home plus a little extra decoration if you wish. Take care when making that you don't use any flammable materials, that you leave plenty of space between the bulb and the shade and that you use a bulb of a suitable power.

If you are buying old lamp bases, have them checked over by an electrician to make sure that they are safe and sound. Most charity shops have to have them tested before they can offer them for sale, but boot sale purchases are made at your own risk. Very old lamps with distinctly archaic flexes should be rewired before you bring them home. This is normally a reasonable economic job, so worth taking them along to your local lamp shop for a quotation.

Mixing and matching and covering lampshades using reclaimed frames is a cheap option too. If you see a pretty-shaped old shade that has seen better days, squirrel it away, stripped of its old fabric and trimmings until you are seeking a different look, or perhaps tempted to make a lampshade Christmas tree (see page 167).

SKIRT AND BELT

This pretty shade is made from material reclaimed
from an old skirt. A simple drawstring channel is
sewn in place at the top and bottom and threaded
through with strong ribbon. The skirt is then popped
over the frame and the ribbons tied together and
tightened until fabric gathers around the shade.
An old belt is used to add definition to the shape
of the frame.

BUTTONS

This stripped frame has been brightened up with
rows of colourful buttons, threaded onto fine wire
and wrapped around the spars at the top and bottom.

BIRDS

Simple leaf shapes and pretty decorative birds have
been stuck to the spars of the frame using a hot glue
gun. Flower shapes, crochet pieces or trimmings
could also be used.

DIP-DYE SHADE

A cylinder of old embroidered sheet fabric with
a drawstring channel at top and bottom, tied with
ribbon and stretched over the frame makes for a plain
shade. To add a splash of colour, mix up a sachet of
cold water dye, according to the instructions on the
packet and immerse the shade half into the mixture.
Leave for a couple of minutes and then lift out,
allow to drain for a moment then dry suspended
over the bowl or on some newspaper.

FESTIVE
AND
SEASONAL

YOU WILL NEED:

....

BASIC PLAIN CRACKERS WITHOUT TRIMMINGS * RULER
* WALLPAPER * SCISSORS * DOUBLE-SIDED TAPE * PRETTY
RIBBONS * LUGGAGE TAG

....

FOR TABLE SETTINGS: WALLPAPER * TAPE MEASURE
* SCISSORS * DOUBLE-SIDED TAPE, STICKY TACK OR
DRAWING PINS * A4 CARDBOARD SHEETS

Vintage wallpaper Christmas crackers and table settings

Making for Christmas-time not only allows you to create some lovely presents, but also offers a brilliant opportunity to add your own vintage style to the Christmas dining table. I struggle with the colour red, so hand-making crackers and table decorations allows me to almost banish this traditional colour from our yuletide palette. Holly berries and robin redbreasts slip through the net, though, to add the odd highlight.

1. Snip any embellishments or ribbons off the crackers if you would like to add your own. Measure the barrel of the cracker and cut a strip of wallpaper the same width and long enough to just overlap when wrapped around the cracker.

2. Place a strip of double-sided tape onto the barrel of the cracker along the seam where it has been made and attach the end of the strip of wallpaper. Wrap it all around the barrel and then secure it in place with another strip of double-sided tape just where it overlaps.

3. Take some pretty ribbon and loop it through the string on the end of a luggage tag. Tie the ribbon around the cracker at both ends of the barrel. Attach a luggage label with a handwritten name to the ribbon before tying if you would like to use the crackers as a name place too.

TABLE SETTINGS

Pretty wallpaper looks lovely as a table runner. Measure the length and width of your table and cut an appropriately sized piece of wallpaper, allowing extra for the paper to tuck under each end. Attach the paper under each end of the table using double-sided sticky tape, sticky tack or even drawing pins to make sure that it is stretched tightly over the table.

Use strips of wallpaper and small pieces of double-sided tape to make pretty paper napkin rings, or stick your chosen vintage wallpaper onto sheets of A4 card with more double-sided tape for an instant set of table mats.

GRADUATED SELECTION OF OLD BELL-SHAPED LAMPSHADES (FROM STANDARD LAMP TO TINY SIDE LIGHT) * ONE OR TWO CYLINDRICAL OLD LAMPSHADES TO MAKE THE TRUNK * PLIERS WITH WIRE CUTTERS * SELECTION OF RIBBONS OR BINDING TAPES, OR PRETTY FABRIC AND A ROTARY CUTTER AND CUTTING MAT FOR MAKING RIBBONS * FABRIC SCISSORS * HOT GLUE GUN OR FABRIC GLUE AND CLOTHES PEGS * FINE FLEXIBLE GARDEN WIRE * PRETTY TRIMMINGS, BAUBLES AND DECORATIONS * PINS

Lampshade Christmas tree

If a real tree is not your style, this old-lampshade version might just fit the bill, whether it is made in minimal all white and decorated with twinkling little pea lights, or covered in metres of bright tinsel, vintage baubles and glitter. If you would like a fill-the-hall-to-the-rafters version, you will need to search out quite a number of shades and be pretty quick at binding the ribbon around the frames.

A little tower of lampshade frames in the corner of my studio provided the original inspiration for this project and a diligent trawl of local charity shops for a couple of weeks yielded enough shades to make a teetering 1.5m tree. This project uses only the frames, so battered and tatty shades that have seen better days are ideal for this purpose. Have a good look inside each shade before you buy to make sure it has a frame inside, rather than just rings of wire. Take the time to look out for the right size and shape frames that will fit together well, but do not worry if the ensemble is not perfect – you can always replace one layer after making if something better comes along. Before you begin, check that the shades will stack, largest first to make a fairly even, graduated Christmas tree shape, with cylindrical lampshade frames at the base to make the trunk.

1. Strip the shades off your frames before you begin, removing as much of the old fabric as you can. The glue used to attach the fabric and trimmings can be fiendishly strong, so grasp the material with pliers and rip it off. Save any pretty trimmings for decorating the tree later.

2. If you are making your own ribbons, cut them from lengths of pretty fabrics, around 2–3cm wide.

3. When your ribbon supply is ready, bind the ribbons around frames. Use a hot glue gun for ease, or fabric glue and clothes pegs and attach the end of a ribbon to a joint of the frame and start to wind it around the spars (you don't need to wait for the glue to dry, just remove the clothes pegs once the fabric glue is set). You can wind each frame with all one colour or chop and change as you go along. When you reach the end of the ribbon, stick it in place as you did before and keep wrapping and attaching lengths of ribbon until all of the frames are covered.

4. Assemble the tree by stacking it up and twisting little lengths of garden wire or tying ribbons nice and tightly around the places where the shades meet.

5. Once the tree is assembled, you can decorate it. Add lengths of reclaimed lampshade trim, bobble edging, chandelier droplets and old baubles. You can glue or tie them in place and use thread or ribbon to attach the baubles. For storage remove the decorations, undo the frames and dismantle the tree. Invert the shades and stack them inside the largest one.

Spruce swags

Bringing in the greenery gives the rooms it hangs in the most refreshing scent - the unmistakably festive aroma of evergreens, glossy holly leaves, pretty berries and trailing leaves. Christmas is a time of year when more is definitely more, so if you do not have enough of your own greenery to cut you can order spruce and ivy from a florist. Christmas tree suppliers often have offcuts that you can buy or take away for free. And if you are cutting from the great outdoors, ensure that you have permission from whoever owns the hedges or land before you prune. Hang the swags over doorways, along mantlepieces or up the banisters. You can decorate them like mini Christmas trees, adding bows and baubles or twinkling lights, or leave the greenery in its natural state. Note that dried spruce burns ferociously, so take care if displaying your swags near fires.

1. Fold the thick rope into thirds and tie each end together with string, about 10cm before the end so you have a loop of rope at each end to hang your swag.

2. Trim your spruce, ivy or Christmas tree branches into short bushy pieces that are around 20–30cm long. Wear gloves if you find the branches too prickly to handle.

3. Lay the tripled rope on a work surface, then place your first greenery piece along the rope at one end with the trimmed stalk end pointing to the middle of the rope. Tie it in place with string by binding it to the rope.

4. Keeping the string on the ball, add another branch next to the first one. (All of the branches need to face the same direction for a smooth, sinuous finished swag.) Wrap the string around this new addition several times, then add the next piece at a slightly different angle just along the rope.

5. Progress along the rope in this way, adding more and more branches, until a bushy tail of foliage begins to form. Tie off the string every so often and start again to ensure that the whole thing is really tight and secure. When you reach the other end of the rope, tie the last couple of pieces on, facing in the opposite direction to that of the rest of the foliage, to make the end tidy.

YOU WILL NEED:

GARDEN WIRE * SELECTION OF GREENERY, SUCH AS HOLLY WITH BERRIES, TRAILING AND BUSHY IVY, CLEMATIS FLOWERS OR OLD MAN'S BEARD, ANY SILVER OR GREY FOLIAGE SUCH AS SAGE, ROSEMARY AND BAY BRANCHES * DRIED ORANGES, DRIED APPLES, CINNAMON STICKS, FIR CONES AND BRANCHES WITH BERRIES OR FRUIT * SECATEURS OR GARDEN SCISSORS * BUCKETS OR CONTAINERS FOR KEEPING FOLIAGE * OASIS FLORAL FOAM CIRCULAR WREATH BASE (NAYLOR BASE RING) * NEWSPAPER (IF NECESSARY) * TWINE OR STRING * FLORIST'S WIRE * VINTAGE BAUBLES OR DECORATIONS AND RIBBONS (OPTIONAL, BUT INTERESTING)

Vintage wreath

Every year in our village we all get together in a fantastic Christmas wreath-making atelier. To the sound of proper old carols, and with clove-spiked mulled cider to keep us warm, and tempting trays of warm homemade mince pies dusted with clouds of icing sugar to fuel us, we dive into buckets of gathered greenery, prickly holly and frothy clematis seed heads, excited in the knowledge that Christmas is just around the corner. We make abundant, overfilled and generous wreaths, hoisting them up onto the hooks in the soft stone walls to admire as we discuss the merits of what makes the perfect wreath. Each wreath is a total reflection of its maker. So gather up your friends, glean your winter greenery and make wreaths together to mark the start of Christmas proper.

1. Begin by gathering up your greenery. Do this over a week or so until you have a good selection, storing cut stems in water. Creating this wreath is a great exercise in making do with what you have – fallen twigs, dried cow parsley stalks, rosemary from the supermarket, hedge trimmings or fake flowers can all be used, so don't worry if you don't have a common brimming with larches or a hedgerow yielding autumn's crop of crab apples.

2. Immerse the oasis in water and soak it really well before you begin. Place the wreath on your work area, covering it with newspaper if necessary. Begin by attaching a strong couple of turns of twine around the oasis and through the hole and tying it off in a loop so you can hang your finished wreath.

3. Start the work on your wreath by adding a good layer of large-leaved foliage, such as bushy ivy, so that you obscure the entire oasis. Snip the end off each little stalk at an angle and remove any lower leaves so you have a clean spike to push into the oasis. Take your time as you arrange the foliage and, from time to time, step back to look at it from all angles to check that you are covering it evenly.

4. Once the first layer is in place, add more frivolous twigs, leaves and stems to the wreath. Odd numbers of eye-catching clusters look better than even numbers, so when adding distinctive foliage or branches with berries, add them in little groups, placed in three or five different positions around the wreath. If you make a mistake and don't like how it looks, simply remove the offending foliage and add something else.

5. When you have plenty of greenery in place, add the final pretty bits to really make the wreath your own. Use florist's wire wrapped around the bases of fir cones or over

cinnamon sticks and dried fruits to attach these embellishments. Hook wire through the loops of little baubles or reclaimed Christmassy trinkets from old decorations. Tie bows in vintage ribbons and wire them in place, too. Hold up your wreath and admire it from all angles, fill any gaps and adjust any unbalanced pieces. When you are happy, you can hang it outside on your door and it should last several weeks if you take it down from time to time and give the oasis a good watering.

TIP To dry oranges for your wreath, slice the whole orange finely through the equator and lay out the pieces on greaseproof paper on a baking tray. Place the tray in a low oven (about 110°C) and leave for a couple of hours until the orange has dehydrated and is just crisp to the touch. Store in an airtight tin until ready to use.

YOU WILL NEED:

TWIGS AND SEASONAL GREENERY
* SECATEURS * DECORATIONS AND
BAUBLES * CHRISTMAS LIGHTS (OPTIONAL)

Decking the halls

To give a picture or a mirror an instant garland, simply tuck branches of holly and trails of ivy behind the frame until you have a little crown behind each one. Remove the first leaves from each stem so that it slips behind the frame easily and hook baubles or Christmas decorations onto the branches or drape them with Christmas lights.

YOU WILL NEED:
....
VINTAGE WALLPAPER SELECTION * DOUBLE-
SIDED TAPE OR GLUE STICK * PAPER SCISSORS

Wallpaper chains

Old-fashioned, charming and a clear marker of the approach of Christmas, these colourful paper chains make a great fireside activity to enjoy with the family in preparation for the big day.

1. Cut a strip of wallpaper across the roll that is about 15cm wide. If you are using double-sided tape, run a strip right the way down the long edge of the strip of paper you have just cut, pressing it firmly in place.

2. Turn the paper strip sideways, then cut across it at 1.5cm intervals to create strips. These will be the links of your chain.

3. Repeat steps 1 and 2 on several different wallpaper designs for some variation in the pattern.

4. Peel away the sticky tape backing on one strip, or add a spot of glue to the end of it, then roll it over and stick one end of it to the other to form a circle. Place the next strip through the centre of the first circle and stick it to close the circle and form the next link in the chain. Repeat the process until a pretty chain begins to form. Make as many chains as you like, in various lengths, depending on your requirements.

YOU WILL NEED:

1 CUP OF SALT (USE DISHWASHER SALT IF YOU ARE MAKING A LARGE BATCH) * 1 HEAPED TABLESPOON OF MIXED SPICE * 1 CUP OF WARM WATER * MIXING BOWL * 2 CUPS OF PLAIN FLOUR, PLUS EXTRA FOR DUSTING * WOODEN SPOON * ROLLING PIN * GINGERBREAD MEN CUTTERS * PEN LID OR SIMILAR (TO CUT HOLES IN THE DOUGH) * BAKING TRAY * GREASEPROOF PAPER * COCKTAIL STICK * WIRE RACK * RIBBON FOR HANGING

Salt dough decorations

This is a project that you might want to do with the children. All you need is a simple salt dough, a couple of biscuit cutters and a little festive cheer. You can make any shape you like, but these gingerbread men always look lovely. Just don't let anyone eat them! The cup measure in the recipe can be any cup – just use the same cup to measure out all the cup quantities.

1. Dissolve the salt and mixed spice in the warm water in a mixing bowl. Add the flour and stir, then knead the whole mixture together on a work surface. Keep going until the dough is soft and pliable, adding more flour or a little sprinkle of water as necessary.

2. When you are happy that the salt dough is well mixed, roll it out onto a floured surface until it is about 0.75cm thick. Use a floured cutter to cut your men out. Now use the lid of a pen to cut tiny circles at the top of the head to create a hole for passing a ribbon through once the shape is baked.

3. Place the shapes onto a baking tray lined with greaseproof paper, spaced evenly, then use a cocktail stick to spike any details onto the gingerbread men. Add eyes, buttons, neckties and clothing details if you wish. Bake on a low heat around 150°C for 45 minutes to two hours, depending on how thick your decorations are. Make sure that they are completely dry before you remove them from the oven, but try not to let them become brown.

3. Remove the shapes from the oven and leave on a wire rack to cool. Thread with ribbon and hang about the home or on the Christmas tree.

YOU WILL NEED:

....

NEWSPAPER * STRIP OF APPROXIMATELY 5CM-WIDE WOOD
CUT TO THE LENGTH OF YOUR FINISHED DECORATION
(ANYTHING FROM ABOUT 30CM UP TO FULL TABLE LENGTH)
* PLENTY OF DRIED FIR CONES OF DIFFERENT SIZES AND
SHAPES * HOT GLUE GUN AND GLUE STICKS, OR FLORIST'S
WIRE AND SECATEURS * LITTLE TWIGS * GOLD PAINT
(OPTIONAL) * PAINTBRUSH (OPTIONAL)

Pine cone mantle

Inspired by the cornicing above doorways in smart houses, these pretty decorations are so lovely, I think it is a shame to keep them just for Christmas. You can collect cones all year long so you are ready for this project in the festive season. Leave the pine cones to dry somewhere warm and they will open up and look even prettier.

You can use a variety of types of pine cone, or stick to just one type. Mature Christmas trees produce dainty cuckoo clock-weights-style cones; alder has clusters of tiny woody cones; larch produces whole branches of papery tiddlers; and Scots pine has generous fat cones. Carefully attaching each cone to a length of wood with florist's wire is a bit of a fiddly and time-consuming business, but arming yourself with a hot glue gun and plenty of glue sticks reduces the construction time significantly. Place the decoration on the dining table, over the mantelpiece, above doors or on windowsills to decorate your home at Christmas-time - or at any time of the year!

1. Lay out the newspaper to protect your work surface, then sit the length of wood on top. Arrange the cones prior to sticking to plan your design. Position the biggest and longest cones in the middle of the length, with a major cone in the centre, and the smaller ones towards the ends of the wood. If you are planning to use your decoration as a table centrepiece, bear in mind that it will have to look good from all sides. If you intend to display it on a mantelpiece, point the cones forwards and, unless you have a mirror on your mantle, you need not worry about the decoration looking so pretty from the back.

2. Stick the major cone to the centre of the length of wood. Squeeze a big blob of hot glue onto the wood, hold the cone upright and press it into the glue for a couple of seconds until it begins to set. Alternatively, wind a length of florist's wire around the base of the cone and twist it in place around the wood.

3. Next, add several more large cones around the first, pointing out like a crown. Work your way along the wooden plank until it is bristling with cones. If you are using glue you can stick more cones on top of the first set to build up intricate patterns. Tuck tiny twigs and pretty branches in between the cones for a more delicate effect, and glue or wire the tiniest cones to float above the rest, if you like.

4. When you are happy with the finished effect, you can highlight some of the cones with a little smudge of gold paint, if you wish.

   TIP To find your piece of wood, try off-cuts at a builders' merchant or use a stout stick from the park.

OASIS FLORAL FOAM TO FIT THE BASE OF YOUR FLOWERPOT * LARGE
FLOWERPOT AND SAUCER * BULBS OR SPRING FLOWERS * A LITTLE
COMPOST * TWIGS * CROCHET OR PAPER FLOWERS * A LITTLE MOSS OR
SOME PEBBLES OR SHELLS (MOSS NEEDS TO BE GATHERED RESPONSIBLY)
* DECORATIONS FOR YOUR TREE, SUCH AS LITTLE FEATHERS, HANGING
EGGS, EASTER TRINKETS, ICED BISCUITS, PINE CONES OR TINY BASKETS
FILLED WITH PRESENTS * STRING, RIBBONS OR PRETTY THREADS

Easter tree

The promise of spring makes Easter such an uplifting time of year and bringing a few of the first buds of the season or some early blossom into your home allows you to enjoy the enticing glimpse of what is to come indoors too. You can dress your Easter tree with gathered trinkets, pretty eggs or edibles, or a mixture of the three. Plan ahead and plant the bulbs that will adorn the base of your tree in the compost at the beginning of the year, adding the leafy twigs at Easter time or instead plant beautiful spring flowers.

1. Place the oasis in the base of the pot - ensure that it reaches about halfway up. Plant your bulbs or flowers in a layer of compost above the oasis. (Bulbs will take several months to get to the flowering stage, but read the instructions that come with each variety to check planting details.) Leave the centre free for adding your twig.

2. When the plants or bulbs are in place and flowering, water the pot really well to saturate the oasis in the base, then plunge your chosen twigs into the centre, right down into the oasis at the base of the pot. You can add little flowers made from paper or fabric to non-flowering twigs, if you like.

3. Cover the top of the compost with a layer of moss, pretty pebbles or shells. Hang the little tree with decorations, strung on ribbons, pretty threads or string.

PAPER AND COLOURED PENCILS (OPTIONAL) * ROYAL ICING MIX * MIXING
BOWL * WOODEN SPOON * FOOD COLOURING * EASTER EGGS OR CHOCOLATES
WITH SMOOTH SURFACES * CUPS (FOR THE EGGS) OR GREASEPROOF PAPER
(FOR THE CHOCOLATES) * FINE RIBBONS (FOR THE EGGS) * ICING TUBE AND
NOZZLES * CRYSTALLISED FLOWERS (AVAILABLE FROM CAKE DECORATING
SHOPS AND GOOD SUPERMARKETS) * TISSUE PAPER OR LITTLE BOXES FOR
WRAPPING * MINI CAKE CASES FOR CHOCOLATES

Icing Easter style

Icing chocolates or chocolate Easter eggs gives you a good excuse, if you need one, for looking out for some vintage kitchenalia for your home. But you don't need a 1950s icing set for this project. You can choose whole Easter eggs to ice, or make your own chocolates or buy any suitable confectionery to decorate.

1. Plan your designs, if you wish, drawing your ideas using coloured pencils. You can simply use initials or write a whole name. You could try little dots, hundreds of tiny spring flowers or intricate Easter-themed patterns. Establish the colourways you intend to use so you can make up the icing in the colours you need.

2. Pour the royal icing mix into a mixing bowl, then make up the icing according to the packet instructions. (It is generally made by adding enough water to create a smooth paste, then beating the mixture with a wooden spoon.) Do not make the paste too thin as the addition of food colouring may water it down further. Divide the icing into several bowls and use food colouring to create the palette of colours you need. Make cones out of greaseproof

paper and use sticky tape to to hold them in place. Snip off a little of the end and drop in a nozzle if you are using one (just snip off the very tip icing without a nozzle) Fill with spoonfuls of your icing mixture.

3. To decorate remove eggs, stand the eggs in cups or line up the chocolates on greaseproof paper. To add a ribbon to your chocolate eggs, dab a little icing onto the top of an egg and press the ribbon down firmly onto it. Wait until it is dry before checking it is firmly attached.

4. For decorating chocolates or eggs, squeeze the icing gently in place following your designs. Use the icing as glue to attach any crystallised flowers. Any mistakes can be wiped away. When you are happy with the results, leave to dry.

5. Pack up the chocolates or the eggs into pretty packaging ready for Easter egg hunts, hanging on your Easter tree (see page 185) or eating alone!

Suppliers

Sarah Moore Vintage
www.sarahmoorevintage.com
01428 707678

Visit Sarah's online home to shop for kits and handmade vintage gifts and homewares. Sign up to the blog for details of courses, vintage finds or more making ideas.

Maxime Jones-Lloyd
www.maxjones-lloyd.co.uk
01428 708078

Darling garden designer, holder of garden-related workshop and maker of the lovely wreaths, swags and mantles in the Festive and Seasonal chapter.

The Mill Shop Online
www.the-millshop-online.co.uk

Super helpful online shop and supplier of really useful extra wide ticking fabrics.

Vintage Home
www.vintage-home.co.uk

Online store packed with original vintage textiles and homewares.

Sanderson
www.sanderson-uk.com

Original producers of fabulous fabrics with a great relaunched vintage collection.

Bellman's Auctioneers
www.bellmans.co.uk

Independent auctioneers with a friendly, knowledgable team to help.

Speedy Stamps
www.speedystamps.co.uk

Next day delivery of stamps of any image, logo or drawing that you would like to upload.

Goose Home and Garden
www.goosehomeandgarden.com

Beautiful original furniture and proper vintage homewares.

The Saleroom
www.the-saleroom.com

Portal that lists lots from auction houses everywhere so you can browse and buy online.

Anthropologie
www.anthropologie.eu

Inspiring original homewares with a vintage vibe.

Cath Kidston
www.cathkidston.co.uk

Great source of new vintage fabrics and bright and cheery homewares.

Annie Sloan Paint
www.anniesloan.com

Fabulous chalk paints and waxes, perfect for vintage projects.

Stable Antiques
www.stableantiques.co.uk

Something for everyone in this warren of an antiques market.

Donna Flower
www.donnaflower.com

Vintage fabrics to buy online from this well-stocked shop.

Cherfold Cottage Flowers
www.cherfoldcottaheflowers.com

Home grown and hand-picked flowers. Find a local florist like Caroline Oleron who will fill your vintage vases with seasonal blooms.

Carboot Junction
www.carbootjunction.com

Dates and details of sales near you.

The Washerwoman
thewasherwoman.blogspot.co.uk

Log on for information on vintage fairs, rag rummages and events.

eBay
www.ebay.co.uk
More vintage listings that you can imagine.

Index

Heartfelt Thanks

Having dream team, Vicky Orchard, Victoria Sawdon and Debi Treloar all together again for this second vintage book has been fabulous. Thanks for all the skill, brilliant design and attention to detail.

And to my home team and friends, thanks for putting up with the vintage habit and for making home a location ever so many times.